UNDERSTANDING COMPUTERS

UNDERSTANDING COMPUTERS

THOMAS H. CROWLEY
Bell Telephone Laboratories
Murray Hill, New Jersey

McGraw-Hill Book Company
New York   St. Louis   San Francisco   Toronto
London   Sydney

UNDERSTANDING COMPUTERS

For Rita

PREFACE

This book originated as a set of notes prepared for a course taught during 1965 in the Union County, New Jersey, Regional Adult School. Students in the course included housewives, businessmen, teachers, bankers, technicians, and a few engineers. Their reasons for attending were varied. Some of the housewives were "computer widows" trying to get a better picture of the rival for their husbands' affections. Many of the business people either had just had computers introduced into their companies or were about to have them introduced. Others were just curious about computers.

My purpose in teaching the course is explained most completely by the discussion in the last chapter of the book. Briefly, I felt that it was not only possible but also worthwhile for nearly any interested person to obtain an accurate basic understanding of the functioning and powers of computers. In particular, I felt that it was not necessary to have any special technical or mathematical training to comprehend such things as memory, programs, symbol manipulation, etc. Consequently, the course, and later the book, assumed no knowledge of mathematics beyond arithmetic or of any concepts from physics or engineering. Experience in teaching the course indicated that such background was not essential and encouraged me to produce this book.

It is, of course, true that for an understanding of the details of the operation of individual circuits in a computer, considerably more study and engineering background is required than this book provides. To get a real grasp of computer programming, it is necessary to actually program, and for some applications of computers, a great deal of mathematical analysis is needed. However, this book should be a good introduction for people such as those in the adult school, for high school seniors or college freshmen who are considering vocational plans, for doctors who are meeting computers in their hospitals, for teachers trying to stay ahead of their bright students, for businessmen trying to understand what their data-processing manager is talking about—in fact, for anybody with limited technical background who has decided to find out what this "computer business" is all about. For those who wish to go further into some aspects, the bibliography contains suggestions for additional reading.

It is not possible to acknowledge all the colleagues from whom I have received substantial advice and aid. However, I would particularly like to thank D. W. Hagelbarger, R. W. Hamming, K. C. Knowlton, E. J. McCluskey, P. G. Neumann, J. R. Pierce, and P. M. Sherman. My thanks to them and to all the others who have been so generous with their suggestions. And, of course, to the secretaries who did all the really hard work, Miss Geraldine Marky and Miss Barbara Bilancioni.

CONTENTS

UNDERSTANDING COMPUTERS

CHAPTER 1

INTRODUCTION

What is a digital computer? What is the difference between a digital computer, a data processor, and a general-purpose scientific computer? How does a computer work? Do computers think? Do computers work only with numbers? Do computers make mistakes?

Everywhere we turn today we seem to run into computers or at least some indication that the computers are "after" us. The bill from the department store comes on a strange piece of stiff paper with a notation "Do not bend, staple, or mutilate." What would happen if we did? (Incidentally, there are reportedly some people who mutilate every such card they receive just to slow down the march of the computers.) Or we get a new checkbook from the bank, and there are strange-looking characters at the bottom of the checks which appear to be in a new language! We pick up a newspaper, and still another prophet is warning us that computers are going to lead to mass unemployment. How are we to evaluate all these reports and get answers to these questions?

Modern computers are large and exceedingly complicated collections of some of the newest and most marvelous devices produced by our highly developed technology. They are designed and used by many specialists whose education may well include a Ph.D. in engineering and probably a great deal of mathematics. It is not too surprising, then, that it is hard to describe a computer in terms that an intelligent layman can understand; any attempt to give a very brief definition is likely to be so superficial as to be misleading. Surprisingly, however, it is possible to describe the organization and operation of a computer in some detail without making use of any background of mathematical or other technical knowledge. And that is just what this book attempts to do.

Why should anyone who has no intention of becoming a computer specialist be interested in understanding how a computer operates? Well, first of all, the questions given in the first paragraph, and many other similar ones, are very interesting and are receiving a lot of attention in the daily press. There is almost no hope of approaching the answers, or even really understanding some of the questions, without a reasonable familiarity with computer operation.

Second, whether our intellectual curiosity is aroused by these questions or not, other basic economic, social, and political questions which relate to computers are hard to avoid. Do computers cause unemployment? In particular, will my job be taken over by a computer? Are computers going to lead us into a "push-button war"? Will computers "dehumanize" our civilization? No matter what our principal occupation is, these questions may arise. A thorough understanding of how computers operate is the first requirement for forming knowledgeable answers.

Finally, the production and use of computers is one of the most rapidly growing parts of our economy. Maybe you will become a computer specialist!

One way to approach the study of computers is through their history, which is a fascinating subject in itself. Since computers are extremely complex and versatile, a great many ideas have played important parts in their development. In addition to these basic ideas, the development of computers has depended heavily on the invention of certain physical devices and tools and on the stimulus provided when people recognized that some manual job was too difficult or time consuming. Unfortunately, it is true of computers, as of most other complex developments, that these three aspects of development did not all occur in a nice, orderly way. All too frequently an idea was available, but physical devices were lacking, or a need was recognized, but no one saw how to use available devices to meet it. (Incidentally, I believe one of the reasons today's technology moves so rapidly is that we make a more determined effort to combine recognized needs, device technology, and theoretical insight or ingenuity.)

More than 5,000 years ago, a need to count was recognized, and somebody had the idea of using first his fingers and then pebbles to help keep track of the count. History is not clear as to whether the need was recognized before or after the idea occurred, but it is clear that the devices—fingers and pebbles—were already available. Since that time, computer development has involved a large number of brilliant ideas, a great deal of effort by many people (much of which was wasted), and contributions from many technical disciplines. The chart on page 4 illustrates schematically how the important devices, ideas, and needs occurred chronologically. Obviously, it is not possible to include every event which had even the slightest relevance to the development of computers, but those which are really basic are shown even though they are not relevant only to computers. Naturally, some of the dates (particularly the ones indicating the recognition of a need) are difficult to establish accurately. In many cases several people developed an idea at about the same time. The chart uses the name usually associated with the development although historians may differ about who should get the credit. Rather than basing our discussion of computers on their historical development, we shall emphasize their functional organization. Consequently, discussion of events on the chart will occur at the point in the book where it is most relevant and comprehensible. Although the connection between computers and some of the chart entries may not be obvious, the discussion to come should make it clear.

Clearly, a description of the operation of a computer in terms of a detailed analysis of the electrical devices from which it is constructed would be useless to anyone who does not have adequate engineering training. Moreover, it is not possible to properly appreciate applications, and possible future applications, of computers merely by reading about large numbers of examples, no matter how interesting they may be. Consequently, in this book we shall identify the important parts of computers, try to get a rough idea of how these rather simple parts operate, and see how they can be put together to produce an amazingly versatile machine.

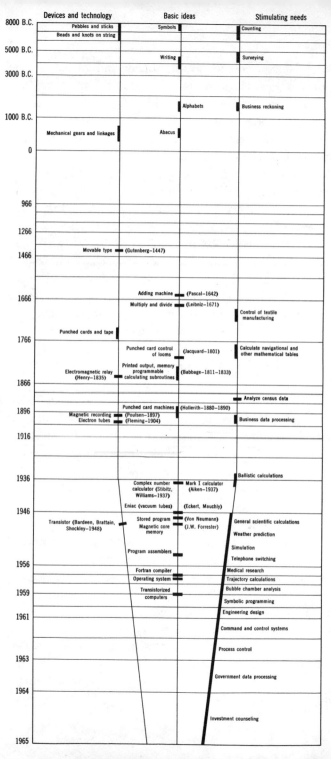

Figure 1-1
Chronological
development
of computers.

Rather than just listing and describing the parts of the machine, we begin by attempting to identify some of the basic functions of a computer as they arise in applications. There is a common misconception that a computer is essentially just a machine for doing arithmetic very rapidly; a computer is very fast, but the arithmetic operations are only a tiny part of its repertoire. Several problems which might be done with a computer are solved manually, and the solutions analyzed, in Chapter 2 in order to identify other basic functions. The operations useful for these manual solutions are available in computers, and each of them is discussed in subsequent chapters. It is possible for one without any engineering background or any mathematics beyond arithmetic to understand quite well just how each of these operations might be carried out in a computer.

In addition to providing a rather detailed description of how computers operate, this book is intended to emphasize some fundamental principles, or characteristics, of computers which are not commonly known or at least not properly appreciated. The first and most important of these is that a computer is a symbol manipulator, not a number manipulator or adding machine. It is not possible to really grasp the generality and power of computers until this difference is appreciated. Chapters 3 and 4 are intended to clarify just what "symbol manipulation" means and at the same time to remove some of the aura of mystery which surrounds computers.

The ability of the computers to process symbols extremely rapidly—most commonly expressed as the ability to add two numbers very rapidly—is, of course, very important, but for many applications the ability to "remember" symbols, i.e., to store them and retrieve them later, is even more important. In other applications the high reliability and accuracy of the computer are the most important characteristics. Chapters 5 to 10 describe the organization and operation of a computer and emphasize these important characteristics.

Although the applications of computers are so varied that only a tiny sample can be discussed in a reasonable time, they can be classified and characterized rather generally. This is done in Chapter 11 by emphasizing which characteristics of computers are most important for particular classes of applications and by emphasizing which characteristics of an application make it most important to use a computer.

The final chapters of the book deal with some of the questions which require an understanding of computers as a basis for their discussion. In Chapter 12 a brief discussion is given of the training and activities of the people who are working with computers. Chapter 13 provides a look into the technical future of computers and describes some of the more exotic applications. Finally, in Chapter 14 some of the really tough questions concerning the consequences for society of the widespread use of computers are considered. It is hoped that at this point the reader will be better able to judge for himself the significance of these questions and will not be disturbed to find that the answers cannot be definitive.

CHAPTER 2

BASIC COMPUTER FUNCTIONS

Let us begin by trying to determine what basic processes might be useful in a computer and what basic parts of the machine would be necessary to carry them out. One way we can approach this is by considering the steps involved in several simple problems. For example, if someone said, "Place all the words on the front page of today's *New York Times* in alphabetical order," how could we proceed? One method would be to take a pair of scissors and cut the page up into small pieces, each containing a single word. We could then spread these pieces out on a big table and sort them into 26 groups according to the first letter of the word on each piece. If we had trouble keeping the groups separated, we could put them in 26 little boxes. We could then arrange the group beginning with the letter *A* by sorting them on the second letter, then the third, etc. (To do the ordering, we might find it convenient to have a listing of the alphabet in front of us, at least, a first grade child or anyone else who didn't know the alphabet would.) After that we could apply the same process to the group beginning with *B*, etc. After placing them all in order on the table, we might take a photograph of them; if we weren't fortunate enough to have a suitable camera, perhaps we'd have to use pen or pencil to copy them somewhat laboriously into a long list.

Before discussing this problem any further,

let's consider a second example. Suppose someone says to us, "Multiply three hundred twenty-five by forty-seven." An item that most of us would find essential is a blackboard or a pencil and paper. Given a blackboard, the first step would be to write down

$$325$$
$$\times 47$$

Then, in succeeding steps we write

325	325	325
× 47	× 47	× 47
2275	2275	2275
	1300	1300
		15275

Figure 2-1   *Using a blackboard for multiplication.*

Finally, we would say, "The answer is fifteen thousand, two hundred seventy-five."

The solutions proposed for both of these problems involved "symbol manipulation"; in the first problem the symbols were words printed on newspaper, and in the second the symbols were numerals written on a blackboard. Processes of this general nature can be carried out in a computer, and, consequently, it will be helpful to us to consider these problems in some detail.

What processes were involved in solving these problems, and what basic facilities were needed? Considering the second problem first, we observe that the blackboard played an important role. We continually wrote symbols on the board, ignored them until some later time when we needed them, and then came back to make use of them, confidently assuming that they would still be there and unchanged. This function of retaining symbols unchanged until they are later retrieved is referred to as *memory;* this is one of the most important basic processes involved in computing, and corresponding to it is one large subdivision of the computer.

Next, we observe that somehow or other we converted some spoken words ("Multiply three hundred twenty-five by forty-seven") into a

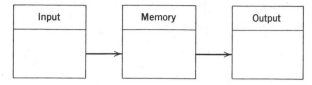

Figure 2-2   *Partial computer block diagram.*

set of symbols written on the blackboard; in other words, we converted symbols from one form (spoken words) into another (chalk dust on the board). We also performed the reverse operation when we gave the answer. This ability to transform symbols from one form to another is a second important process; it goes on within a computer in many ways, but one particularly important operation which makes use of it is illustrated in this example. This operation is referred to as *input-output,* and the part of the computer which carries out this operation is referred to as *input-output equipment.* In our example this "equipment" includes our ear, mouth, hand, part of our brain, and the stick of chalk since they were used in this process of transforming words into chalk symbols, and vice versa. Since we may well need different pieces of equipment for these operations, we can represent the parts of the computer that we have identified so far in a diagram like Figure 2-2.

Another basic process involved in the numerical example is represented by the step in which we considered the two symbols 5 and 7, multiplied them in our head to get 35 and wrote 5 down on the first line below the problem. In other words, we combined two of the symbols to produce a third. At a later step we combined two symbols, for example, 7 and 0, by adding them to produce a third. As you might guess, a lot of operations within the computer involve this basic process of manipulating one, two, or more symbols and producing another symbol as a result. We call the part of the computer in which these operations are carried out the *processor.* Our block diagram of the computer now looks like Figure 2-3.

Incidentally, another basic process which we have not identified before is indicated by the arrows on this diagram. They represent the *transmission,* or transfer, of symbols from one part of the machine to another. The equipment used for this purpose is referred to as *data links* or *data busses.*

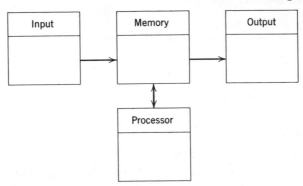

Figure 2-3   Partial computer block diagram.

There is one rather subtle part of the processing which might easily escape our attention. Why did we multiply first the 5 and 7, then the 2 and 7, etc.? After finishing the multiplications, why did we start adding the intermediate results? In other words, how was the order of the operations controlled? Clearly, some part of our brain was carrying out this function of directing the entire computation; the corresponding part of the computer is called the *control unit*. After adding this unit the basic organization of the computer is that shown in Figure 2-4.

Having listed five different processes used in solving the second problem, we can examine the first example to see whether the same processes can be identified there—wouldn't we all be surprised if they couldn't! However, they are all there; you might find it interesting to

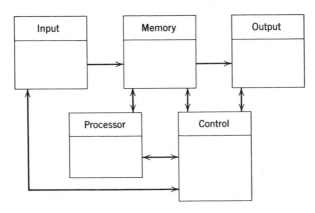

Figure 2-4   Computer block diagram.

Table 2-1 Basic processes involved in alphabetizing words on newspaper page

	Equipment	Process
Input	Ear, brain	Convert words into instructions in brain
	Scissors	Cut page into pieces
Memory	Boxes	Store individual pieces
	Listing of alphabet	Store order of alphabet
Processor	Brain, hands	Move pieces between boxes
Output	Camera or paper and pencil	Make record
Control	Brain	Order steps of processing

try to identify some of them before looking at Table 2-1. Incidentally, the basic process of symbol transmission was also represented by the moving of the pieces of paper from one box (or position) to another on the table top.

We have established that these two examples make use of some common processes, but they're definitely different in detail. Most people would have no trouble doing either job since our brain (the control unit) can specify the appropriate sequence of steps depending on which job has been assigned. Some computers, called *special-purpose computers,* can carry out only one sequence of steps; like a dog trained to do just one trick, they could be built to do either of these jobs but not both. A *general-purpose computer* can carry out many different sequences of steps and could do both these jobs (as well as many others). In order to do this, however, the control unit must be given instructions concerning what sequence of steps is to be carried out. This set of instructions is called the *program.* Providing the right program is one of the hardest and, at the same time, most interesting problems in using a computer. There are very few truly special-purpose computers used these days, and in this book we shall discuss only general-purpose, or programmable, computers. (The term special-purpose computer is also frequently used in a confusing manner to mean a programmable computer which would be inefficient if used to do certain operations.)

In later chapters we shall define each of the basic processes more carefully, discuss the corresponding parts of the computer in some detail, and describe the preparation of a computer program. However, before we do that, something which we have been talking about rather casually needs to be considered more carefully: What are the "symbols" to which we have been referring? In the first example, the symbols were groups of letters made up of ink deposited on paper. In the second example, we were using chalk dust placed on a blackboard in the shapes of the set of symbols consisting of the ten digits 0, 1, 2, 3, 4, 5, 6, 7, 8, 9 and the two special characters $\times$ and_____(underline). For both problems our solution was obtained by manipulating these symbols according to an appropriate set of rules. Clearly, if we are to carry out similar computations, there must be something in the computer to correspond to symbols of this sort. What is used? In other words, what does a data processor process? In the next chapter this question is answered.

CHAPTER 3

WHAT IS BEING PROCESSED?

Since a computer is a real, physical machine, it can manipulate only concrete, physical objects, or, to say it in another way, it can only make changes in some physical condition. Consequently, the answer to the question, "What is being processed?", cannot be anything like "a number" since a number is an abstraction; the symbols being processed must be something physical. Let us begin by considering a simple machine which is distantly related to a computer.

You are probably familiar with the elementary adding machines which are seen on desk tops or incorporated in cash registers. Although these machines are usually thought of as adding numbers, you are probably aware that the actual processing consists of changing the position of many small cogged wheels. In most machines these wheels have 10 cogs, each of which can be identified so that, if a marker is placed somewhere around the circumference of the wheel, the wheel can take any of 10 distinct positions with respect to the marker. In practice the marker is frequently a cog on another wheel. In these machines the symbols, or physical conditions, that are manipulated are actually the positions of wheels; each wheel can be in any one of 10 positions so that only one wheel is necessary for 10 different symbols. Figure 3-1 shows how three wheels can be used to represent the number 325.

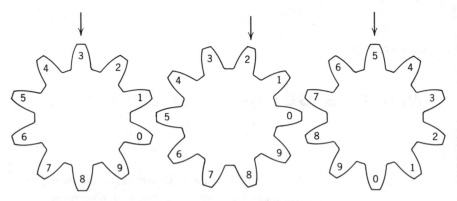

Figure 3-1   Cogged wheels storing numeral 325.

Another familiar device which produces symbols is a traffic light. Instead of 10 possible conditions which we can distinguish, there are only 3; the light is red, or it is green, or it is yellow. By changing the light from one condition to another, large numbers of cars can be effectively controlled—although it's getting harder and harder! Still another device producing symbols is the light on top of a taxi. The light has just two distinguishable conditions; it is off or it is on. If the light is on, we assume the taxi is available, and if the light is off, we assume the taxi is already taken.

In modern computers many different physical objects or conditions are used in addition to, or in place of, lights and cogged wheels. An example with which many of you may be familiar in the form of an ordinary door buzzer is called an electromagnetic *relay*. The simplest form of a relay consists of two metallic contacts mounted on springs immediately above a coil of wire. These contacts normally do not touch; however, if the coil of wire is magnetized by causing an electric current to flow through it, the contacts are closed by the resulting magnetic force. This device is like the taxi light in that it can be in either of two conditions, namely, contacts open or contacts closed for the relay, and light off or light on for the taxi light.

Another type of "device" which you have all seen is the ubiquitous punched card. Such cards can be thought of as subdivided into many areas with each of these areas being either unmodified, or modified by having a hole punched in it. Each area thus is a device which can be in either of two conditions, i.e., punched or unpunched. The punched card is unlike the relay and the light in that it is not possible to go back and forth between the two conditions since the hole cannot be "unpunched."

In modern computers it is very common to use devices which involve electric or magnetic conditions instead of the mechanical conditions involved in the above devices—several examples will be mentioned in later sections. Naturally, some background in the understanding of electric and magnetic phenomena is necessary to understand how these conditions are manipulated and to design a device which can make use of them. However, there is nothing particularly mysterious or more powerful about these devices; they are used simply because they are inexpensive and because they can be changed from one condition to another very rapidly. Operation of these devices in a computer involves manipulations similar to opening and closing relay contacts, turning lights on and off, rotating a cog wheel, or punching a hole in a piece of cardboard.

Let us try to be precise now about our meaning of the word *symbol*. Computers are made up of many different kinds of devices, and each of these devices can be in two or more distinguishable conditions. We shall refer to a device in a particular condition as a *symbol*. A device can therefore produce as many symbols as it has distinguishable conditions. Thus, a wheel with 10 cogs can produce 10 symbols, whereas a light, or a pair of relay contacts, can produce only 2 symbols. Computers can be, and have been, built by using devices which can take on 2, or 3, or 10, or any specific number of conditions. It happens that at the present time the most reliable, the cheapest, and the fastest devices are similar to relay contacts in that they have just two easily distinguished conditions; consequently, machines are made by using large numbers of such devices (hereafter called *binary* devices).

Notice that our usage of the word symbol differs slightly from ordinary usage in that we are not specifying that the symbol must have some particular meaning or interpretation. Obviously, manipulating symbols within a computer would serve no useful purpose if they had no meaning, i.e., if they did not "symbolize" something. In the next chapter, we shall be discussing various meanings and interpretations of these symbols, and we shall find that computer symbols have different interpretations at different times. It will become clear as we go along that there always is some useful interpretation of the symbols within a computer, but since this interpretation is not unique, we shall consider it as being specified by the symbol and the context rather than just by the symbol.

We shall need some way to represent the two conditions into which binary devices can be put so that we can talk about them and keep track of the symbol they are producing. We could have a special notation for each device; i.e., we might draw a little picture of relay contacts in either the open or closed condition, draw a picture of a punched card to indicate whether or not a hole was present, use some other picture to represent two different types of magnetic condition, and so on, as is done in Figure 3-2. However, for our purposes it will only be necessary to recall that each of these binary devices must be in either of two conditions, i.e., is producing either of two symbols, and to distinguish between these two. Thus, we can greatly simplify the notation by ignoring the type of device which is involved and always

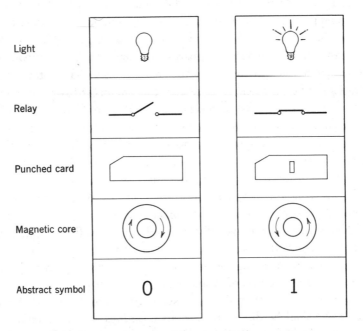

Figure 3-2   *Possible notations for binary symbols.*

represent the two conditions by the marks 1 and 0. One condition of a binary device will be denoted arbitrarily as 1, and the other condition will be denoted as 0. Any other two marks would do just as well for our purpose; for example, $+$ and $-$ could be used. Note that the 1 and 0 are not being used as numerals; they are being used as symbols which we can easily distinguish. We are using just one device, ink on paper, to represent all the different kinds of devices used in computers. We shall frequently refer to the marks 0 and 1 as symbols (which they are, since they are two of the many ways of putting ink on paper), and it will usually not be necessary to recall that they are just representing the actual computer symbols.

Although possible, it would be very clumsy to describe computers in terms of only two symbols. In fact, it is frequently simpler to consider a group of binary devices as a single "super device" which can be in more than two conditions. For example, a super device consisting of two binary devices can be in any one of four conditions and thus produces four symbols. The natural way to extend our notation is to represent these four symbols as 00, 01, 10, and 11. If the super device is made up of three binary devices, we shall use a row of three 0s or 1s to represent the symbols produced by the device and similarly for any other size super device. For example, 1111 will be a symbol which represents one possible condition of a super device made up of four specified binary devices. This symbol is not a number (we shall frequently call it a *word*) and does not imply that these devices are located in a row or are even of the same kind. It is simply a symbol representing one possible condition out of the 16 different conditions possible for such a super device. (An easy way to see that there are 16 different conditions possible is to write down all possible combinations of four 1s and 0s. If you don't find 16, look a little harder because you've missed some!)

We shall frequently refer to a single one of the 1s or 0s in a word as a *bit*. For example, the symbol 11110010 will be referred to as an 8-bit word, and the bit in the third position from the right is a 0.

It is easily established that an n-bit word can produce 2^n, that is,

$$\overbrace{2\times2\times\ldots\times2}^{n},$$ different symbols. A super device made up of just 20 binary devices produces 1,048,576 (which is $2\times2\times2\times2\times2\times2\times2\times2\times2\times2\times2\times2\times2\times2\times2\times2\times2\times2\times2\times2$) different symbols!

As previously mentioned, the symbols which are being manipulated in a computer must be interpreted in some meaningful way in order for the processing to have any value. It is this interpretation of the symbols as "data" or "information" which leads to the terms *data processor* and *information processor*. In the next chapter, we shall see how such interpretations can be made.

CHAPTER 4

INTERPRETATION OF SYMBOLS

We don't really know when men first began to make use of symbols, but it certainly must have occurred in prehistoric times. Our first certain evidence of the use of symbols is provided by the invention of writing. Like many other inventions, this one took place over a period of time and was conceived independently by different peoples. The Egyptians developed their system of hieroglyphics over the approximate period of 4000 to 2000 B.C. They began by using pictograms, which were sketchy pictures of the thing represented. These gradually evolved into images with less pictorial value and were associated with a unique word of the language. Ultimately they associated these symbols with the elementary sounds making up the words. However, it was not until about 1200 B.C. that the Phoenicians and Greeks developed the first bona fide alphabet.

We are so used to identifying a symbol with its meaning that we sometimes overlook the fact that no symbol has any "meaning" or interpretation except by convention. For example, the symbol 8 has no intrinsic connection with any number. People have simply agreed by convention that that symbol will be used to represent a particular number. Of course, some symbols are chosen to be quite suggestive of their interpretation, e.g., the Roman numeral III or the skull-and-crossbones symbol for poison, but the meaning is still really a matter of convention.

A second important observation is that it is not necessary that a symbol have a unique interpretation. For example, consider the symbol X. If we happen to be talking about letters of the alphabet, we shall all interpret this as the twenty-fourth letter of the alphabet. On the other hand, if we had happened to be talking about Roman numerals, we would have interpreted it as the symbol representing the number 10, or if we had happened to be talking about arithmetic operations, we would have recognized it as a symbol for multiplication. In any particular situation, as long as it is clear which set of possible meanings we are considering, we can interpret the symbol unambiguously. If, however, we become confused about what set of possible interpretations we are considering at any given moment, we might incorrectly interpret the symbol to be, for example, a letter of the alphabet when it was intended to be a multiplication sign.

When we think of symbols, we tend to think first of symbols drawn on paper and interpreted as such abstract concepts as letters or numbers. However, we use many other symbols in our daily lives. For example, a traffic light is a device which produces three symbols depending on whether the light is red, green, or yellow. By convention we agree to interpret these as meaning stop, go, and proceed with caution. In this case the symbols are interpreted as concrete instructions rather than abstract concepts, but their interpretations are still just a matter of convention. Actually, we could use any device with three distinguishable conditions for a traffic signal and agree on a particular interpretation for every intersection where the devices are used. However, it is much simpler and more convenient to use the same device and agree on the same interpretation in all places or at least use as few different devices and interpretations as possible. (In fact, different devices and interpretations are used in some places, and it behooves a person driving in a strange state or country to do a little checking on the interpretation of signals.) In addition to other kinds of traffic signals, many other symbols are very familiar to us, for example, barber poles, taxi lights or flags.

The general process by which conventions for interpretations of symbols are made is illustrated quite well by the preceding examples.

In any specific situation we are usually concerned with some particular set, or group, of concepts, e.g., letters of the alphabet, numbers, traffic signals, or arithmetic operations; a particular symbol is then interpreted as specifying a particular one out of this set. The process of establishing the correspondence between particular symbols and particular meanings in the set of meanings is essentially arbitrary and can be done in many ways. A symbol used in this way to specify precisely one out of a set of possible meanings is said to convey *information*; consequently, machines for processing these symbols are sometimes called *information processors*. There is a very elaborate theory available to measure amounts of information, to determine whether a process loses information, and to find ways of using a particular set of symbols to carry a maximum amount of information. When the information that is conveyed is the result of a series of experiments or events of some sort, the symbols are frequently referred to as *data,* and so machines for processing these symbols are sometimes called *data processors.* For example, the data might record the names and the number of hours worked in a particular week for each person on the payroll of some company; these data could be used in the process of making up the company's weekly payroll. We shall not need to discuss any of the details of information theory (although it is a very interesting theory), but it will be useful to consider in more detail the interpretations of symbols in the computer.

Symbols within the computer are interpreted according to conventions established by the computer designers and computer users. Since different sets of meanings are involved at various points in the operation of a computer, a symbol may have different interpretations at different times. Specifically, at one time a symbol might be interpreted as a number; at another time the same symbol will be interpreted as a letter; and at still another time it might be interpreted as an instruction to carry out some sort of operation. In each case, as long as it is clear at that moment which interpretation is to be made, no difficulties arise.

How can we ensure that the designers and users of the computer agree on the interpretation of the symbols? One rather obvious way is simply to write down in a table the different symbols and their interpretation; this table is then made available to all the computer users. In

| Table 4-1 | | Table 4-2 | |
Six-bit alphameric code		Seven-bit alphameric code	
0	000000	0	0000000
1	000001	1	1000001
2	000010	2	1000010
3	000011	3	0000011
4	000100	4	1000100
5	000101	5	0000101
6	000110	6	0000110
7	000111	7	1000111
8	001000	8	1001000
9	001001	9	0001001
[	001010	[	0001010
#	001011	#	1001011
@	001100	@	0001100
:	001101	:	1001101
>	001110	>	1001110
?	001111	?	0001111
(space)	010000	(space)	1010000
A	010001	A	0010001
B	010010	B	0010010
C	010011	C	1010011
D	010100	D	0010100
E	010101	E	1010101
F	010110	F	1010110
G	010111	G	0010111
H	011000	H	0011000
I	011001	I	1011001
&	011010	&	1011010
.	011011	.	0011011
]	011100	]	1011100
(	011101	(	0011101
<	011110	<	0011110
\	011111	\	1011111
↑	100000	↑	1100000
J	100001	J	0100001
K	100010	K	0100010
L	100011	L	1100011
M	100100	M	0100100
N	100101	N	1100101
O	100110	O	1100110
P	100111	P	0100111
Q	101000	Q	0101000

Table 4-1
Six-bit alphameric code

Table 4-2
Seven-bit alphameric code

Symbol	Six-bit code	Symbol	Seven-bit code
R	101001	R	1101001
–	101010	–	1101010
$	101011	$	0101011
*	101100	*	1101100
)	101101	)	0101101
;	101110	;	0101110
'	101111	'	1101111
+	110000	+	0110000
/	110001	/	1110001
S	110010	S	1110010
T	110011	T	0110011
U	110100	U	1110100
V	110101	V	0110101
W	110110	W	0110110
X	110111	X	1110111
Y	111000	Y	1111000
Z	111001	Z	0111001
←	111010	←	0111010
,	111011	,	1111011
%	111100	%	0111100
=	111101	=	1111101
"	111110	"	1111110
!	111111	!	0111111

order to make up such a table, the designer must decide what set of interpretations he wants to consider and what symbols he wants to use (i.e., how many bits in each word), and then he must choose a particular correspondence between them. One commonly used representation is shown in Table 4-1.

In this case the designers have decided to make available as interpretations the letters of the English alphabet (uppercase only), the 10 digits, and some additional special characters (comma, period, dollar sign, etc.). Since a 5-bit word would only allow 32 (which is $2\times2\times2\times2\times2$) distinct interpretations, it is clear that at least 6 bits are necessary to provide for the 26 letters and 10 digits. Consequently, the designers settled on a 6-bit word and then chose enough special characters to exhaust the 64 different symbols. For convenience, this whole set of characters is referred to as the *alphameric*, or *alphanumeric*, characters.

Why were these characters chosen and not others? This is one of the many arbitrary decisions which must be made by computer designers. Clearly, if the computer is to be used for problems such as the first one discussed in Chapter 2 (alphabetizing all the words on a newspaper page), it is necessary to be able to represent English letters. However, it is not absolutely necessary that the words be distinguished when they are capitalized; hence the decision not to include lowercase letters. Since we may want to use the computer for some business data processing, a dollar sign is likely to be useful. Other special characters are chosen on the basis of similar arguments related to possible applications.

Let us digress slightly at this point and consider very briefly an alternative correspondence shown in Table 4-2. A 7-bit word is used for each character in this table, and a comparison of the two tables shows that in Table 4-2 the last 6 bits of the symbol for any particular character form the symbol corresponding to the same character in Table 4-1! Why is the 7-bit word used when a 6-bit word is sufficient? A close examination of the symbols in Table 4-2 will provide a clue. Note that every symbol contains an even number of 1s. Thus, Table 4-2 was formed from Table 4-1 by adding to each symbol an initial bit, which was chosen to be 1 or 0 as necessary to make the symbol have an even number of 1s.

This particular type of representation is one of the simplest examples of an *error-detecting* representation (sometimes called an error-detecting encoding). At various times in the computer processing of such symbols, the computer counts the number of 1s in each symbol. If any symbol has an odd number of 1s, a mistake has occurred, and a warning message is provided. Of course, it is possible that 2 bits in a symbol might be in error so that the total number of 1s is still even, and the error would be undetected. However, if the number of errors which occur is very small, it is very, very unlikely that there will be two errors in one word. This type of representation can be extended so that errors cannot only be detected, they can also be corrected. The correction which is made depends on the fact that it is very unlikely that many errors will be made in the same word. In the very remote possibility that a number of errors do occur in the same word, the correction may be in error; for example, multiple errors may change one word into another word, which would apparently require no correction but would in fact be incorrect.

Later on, in our discussion of applications, we shall find that it is extremely important that the computer be able to perform many millions of operations without making any undetected errors. Since a computer is made up of devices which *can* fail, and errors *do* occur, it is only by making clever use of techniques of this sort that the necessary high reliability is obtained. We shall not describe in detail all the ways in which this method of error detecting, or similar ones, are used in the computer, but it is important to note that such techniques are available and that they increase the reliability of the machine by many orders of magnitude. Of course, occasional undetected errors are made by the computer, but these are few in number compared with the errors made by people doing similar problems.

Now let us return to our discussion of the interpretation of symbols. Using the agreed-upon symbols of Table 4-1 for the alphanumeric characters, we can construct symbols for strings of these characters and thus form symbols for arbitrary numbers of English words. For example, the number 763 is represented by 000111 000110 000011, and the word THE is represented by 110011 011000 010101. Because we have symbols representing commas, periods, and spaces, we can easily construct symbols representing sentences, paragraphs, or even complete books. For example, Figure 4-1 shows a sonnet which has warmed the heart of many a pretty girl. Although the meaning is unchanged when it is written in this form, I'll agree that it does lose something in translation.

Similarly, by using the period as a decimal point, we can represent arbitrarily large or small numbers. Clearly, just agreeing on this one table of interpretations provides us with an extremely flexible and powerful way of representing abstract concepts (numbers and natural-language words are really abstract concepts) using only the symbols available within the computer. Moreover, if symbols within the computer were always interpreted according to the one table, there would never be any ambiguity as to the meaning of the symbol.

However, there are good reasons for using other correspondences in addition to this one. In particular, it is common to use several different representations for numbers; one of the chief reasons for this is

011000 100110 110110 010000 010100 100110 010000 011001 010000

100011 100110 110101 010101 010000 110011 011000 010101 010101

001111 100011 010101 110011 010000 100100 010101 010000 010011

100110 110100 100101 110011 010000 110011 011000 010101 010000

110110 010001 111000 110010 011011 011001 010000 100011 100110

110101 010101 010000 110011 011000 010101 010101 010000 110011

100110 010000 110011 011000 010101 010000 010100 010101 100111

110011 011000 010000 010001 100101 010100 010000 010010 101001

010101 010001 010100 110011 011000 010000 010001 100101 010100

010000 011000 010101 011001 010111 011000 110011 010000

100100 111000 010000 110010 100110 110100 100011 010000

010011 010001 100101 010000 101001 010101 010001 010011 011000 111011

010101 011011 010010 101001 100110 110110 100101 011001 100101 010111

Figure 4-1   Sonnet in computer language (translated from original by
*   T. H. Crowley).*

that the representation of numbers using the correspondence of Tables 4-1 or 4-2 is unnecessarily wasteful of bits. For example, to represent a number between 0 and 999, 18 bits are required, i.e., a 6-bit symbol for each of the three digits in the number. However, since there are 1,024 different 10-bit symbols ($1,024=2\times2\times2\times2\times2\times2\times2\times2\times2\times2$), any integer from 0 to 1,023 could be represented by using only 10 bits. This is a saving of 8 bits, almost 50 percent.

One way to correct this would be to construct another table similar to Table 4-1 and simply list all the integers from 0 to 1,023 with an arbitrarily chosen 10-bit symbol corresponding to each. However, if this correspondence is defined more methodically, it is both easier for the user to remember and simpler to design the computer. As a matter of fact, this regularity is one of the chief reasons that we prefer our modern system of representing numbers over that of the Romans. Although Roman numerals are a precise and well-defined way to represent numbers, they are formed in a much less methodical and much more arbitrary way than our numerals. Consequently, we find them much harder to do arithmetic with, to remember, and so on. The introduction of positional notation about 2000 B.C. made it much easier for people to use symbols to represent numbers, and a very similar system is used in computers to simplify the construction of the computer.

Just to be specific, let us consider a symbol, or word, which is made up of 10 bits. As mentioned above, this allows the representation of 1,024 integers. If we wanted to represent more than a thousand numbers, we would have to use longer words. (It is not unusual today to use 70 or 100 bits; this allows the representation of more than a trillion trillion numbers.) Let's say for our purposes that a thousand numbers is enough so that we can get by with just 10 bits. One very common way in which these symbols are used to represent the integers from 0 to 1,023 is the following: Represent the integer N as the 10-bit symbol *abcdefghij* (where each of the letters must be replaced by either 1 or 0) when

$$N=a\times512+b\times256+c\times128+d\times64+e\times32+f\times16+g\times8+h\times4+i\times2+j\times1$$

(Note: If $a=1$, then $a\times512=1\times512=512$. If $a=0$, then $a\times512=0\times512=0$.) For example,

5 is represented by 0000000101 since

$$0 \times 512 + 0 \times 256 + 0 \times 128 + 0 \times 64 + 0 \times 32 + 0 \times 16 + 0 \times 8 + \underline{1 \times 4}$$
$$+ 0 \times 2 + \underline{1 \times 1} = 4 + 1 = 5$$

16 is represented by 0000010000 since

$$0 \times 512 + 0 \times 256 + 0 \times 128 + 0 \times 64 + 0 \times 32 + \underline{1 \times 16} + 0 \times 8 + 0 \times 4$$
$$+ 0 \times 2 + 0 \times 1 = 16 + 0 = 16$$

1,023 is represented by 1111111111 since

$$1 \times 512 + 1 \times 256 + 1 \times 128 + 1 \times 64 + 1 \times 32 + 1 \times 16 + 1 \times 8 + 1 \times 4$$
$$+ 1 \times 2 + 1 \times 1 = 1{,}023$$

This representation is referred to as *binary notation* because it requires only two symbols 0 and 1 (although they are used in groups, as above, so as to produce more symbols) and because the numbers 512, 256, 128, etc., used in setting up the correspondence, are powers of 2, that is, $512 = 2^9$, $256 = 2^8$, $128 = 2^7$, etc. Binary notation is said to have the *base* 2. Ordinary *decimal notation* is set up in exactly the same manner except that it uses base 10 (ten) instead of base 2. Thus, the integer N is represented as abc (where each of the letters must be replaced by 0,1,2,3,4,5,6,7,8, or 9) when $N = a \times 100 + b \times 10 + c \times 1$. For example, the three hundred fifty-first integer is represented (when we are using decimal notation) by the numeral 351 since $351 = 3 \times 100 \mid 5 \times 10 + 1 \times 1$.

A serious difficulty with the binary number system, as we have defined it, is that it represents only whole numbers; certainly we must be able to represent fractions for some computer applications. In decimal notation we use a *decimal point* to extend the representation to include decimal fractions. For example, 351.27 represents $3 \times 100 + 5 \times 10 + 1 \times 1 + 2 \times \frac{1}{10} + 7 \times \frac{1}{100}$. In general, the digits to the right of the decimal point represent multiples of $\frac{1}{10}$, $\frac{1}{100}$, $\frac{1}{1{,}000}$, etc.

In the same way, by using bits to the right of a *binary point*, we can extend binary notation to include the representation of fractions. For example, 11.101 represents $1 \times 2 + 1 \times 1 + 1 \times \frac{1}{2} + 0 \times \frac{1}{4} + 1 \times \frac{1}{8} = 3\frac{5}{8}$. Here are some other examples to practice on:

111.111 represents $1 \times 4 + 1 \times 2 + 1 \times 1 + 1 \times \frac{1}{2} + 1 \times \frac{1}{4} + 1 \times \frac{1}{8} = 7\frac{7}{8}$
100.001 represents $\underline{1 \times 4} + 0 \times 2 + 0 \times 1 + 0 \times \frac{1}{2} + 0 \times \frac{1}{4} + \underline{1 \times \frac{1}{8}} = 4\frac{1}{8}$
.000001 represents
$$0 \times \frac{1}{2} + 0 \times \frac{1}{4} + 0 \times \frac{1}{8} + 0 \times \frac{1}{16} + 0 \times \frac{1}{32} + \underline{1 \times \frac{1}{64}} = \frac{1}{64}$$

Using a binary point gets around the difficulty of expressing fractions, but now we must face up to the fact that our symbols in the computer are composed of only 0s and 1s, and we do not really have a binary point. This appears to be a serious difficulty, but it is overcome easily by again making use of an agreement between the computer designers and users. The computer designers simply decide that everyone shall act as though there is a binary point at the right end—or the left end—or the center—of the word. For example, if 10-bit words were to be used in the computer, it might be agreed that the binary point was to be between the fifth and sixth bits. Having established this convention, we now have a number system which uses only binary symbols for representing mixed numbers (fractions and integers). Here are some examples:

$5\frac{1}{2}$ is represented by 0010110000 since

$$0\times16+0\times8+1\times4+0\times2+1\times1+1\times\tfrac{1}{2}+0\times\tfrac{1}{4}+0\times\tfrac{1}{8}$$
$$+0\times\tfrac{1}{16}+0\times\tfrac{1}{32}=4+1+\tfrac{1}{2}=5\tfrac{1}{2}$$

$\frac{3}{4}$ is represented by 0000011000 since

$$0\times16+0\times8+0\times4+0\times2+0\times1+1\times\tfrac{1}{2}+1\times\tfrac{1}{4}+0\times\tfrac{1}{8}+0$$
$$\times\tfrac{1}{16}+0\times\tfrac{1}{32}=\tfrac{1}{4}+\tfrac{1}{2}=\tfrac{3}{4}$$

Having successfully found a way to represent fractions, we now come up against another difficulty. Since we are now using half the symbol for representing the whole number and half for representing the fractional part of the number, we have reduced the size of the largest number which can be represented. Correspondingly, we have limited the smallest number which can be represented, since the more bits there are to the right of the binary point, the smaller the number which can be represented. The largest number which can be represented with our 10-bit word is $31\frac{31}{32}$ and the smallest is $\frac{1}{32}$. By increasing the length of the symbol to 20, 30, or even 40 bits, these effects are reduced. However, there are practical limits to how much the word size can be increased, and in any case half the word is being wasted if we are interested in only very large or very small numbers.

It is possible to use multiple words to represent either bigger or smaller numbers in this system provided we keep very careful account of where the binary point is located in these symbols. However, keeping track of the binary point is very difficult to do in many computations, and the multiple words are clumsy (and expensive) to use. Consequently, still another representation of numbers is needed! We shall call this third way of representing numbers *wide-range notation* since its chief advantage is the facility for representing very large as well as very small numbers.

We shall define wide-range notation for 15-bit words, and it will be obvious that similar definitions can be given for other word lengths. We shall consider the 15-bit word as made up of three parts of 1, 5, and 9 bits, respectively. The last 9 bits will be interpreted as representing an integer in ordinary binary notation. Hence we can think of these bits as a binary number with the binary point initially located just to the right of the rightmost bit. Now we use the first two parts of the symbol to specify where the binary point should be moved. If the first bit is a 1, the binary point is moved to the right; if the first bit is a 0, the binary point is moved to the left. The remaining 5 bits represent a binary number which tells us how much the binary point is moved. Thus, if these bits represent 17 in binary notation, the binary point is moved 17 places to the right or left depending on whether the first bit is a 1 or a 0. Sounds complicated? Let's look at some examples.

Consider the symbol 100011000000111. The three pieces are 1 00011 000000111. The second piece represents the number 3 and since the first bit is a 1, the binary point is to be moved 3 places to the right. Therefore, this wide-range symbol represents the same number as the binary symbol 000000111000 (which is 56 in ordinary decimal notation). Here are some additional examples:

Wide range	Binary	Decimal
1 11111 111111111	111111111000000000000000-000000000000000. (Binary point was moved 31 places to the right.)	Approximately 2 trillion
0 11111 111111111	.000000000000000000000011-1111111 (Binary point was moved 31 places to the left.)	Approximately .0000005
1 00000 100000111	100000111. (Binary point was moved 0 places to the right.)	263

These examples certainly indicate that both very large and very small numbers can be represented using this notation. Along with this advantage, we find certain disadvantages. For one thing, some numbers have more than one representation in this system; for example, zero is represented by any symbol in which the last 9 bits are 0. For another thing, the numbers which can be represented are not uniformly spaced between the smallest and the largest numbers which can be represented. However, by using either binary notation or wide-range notation, as appropriate to a particular application, the computer user has available the advantages of both. Although I know of no computer which uses a representation exactly like our wide-range notation, many computers use a representation called *floating point notation,* which is very closely related. It is essentially the same as wide-range notation although it differs in some details.

To those familiar with negative numbers, it is probably obvious that some applications of computers require their use. (For those unfamiliar with negative numbers, let me just say that they are used by the bank when you overdraw your account.) There are several representations commonly used—the simplest just reserves the first bit of the symbol to specify whether the number represented is positive or negative. Thus, we could modify both the binary notation and the wide-range notation by adding an extra bit at the beginning of the word with the convention that the number is positive if this bit is a 1 and negative otherwise. We shall not be discussing any applications in which negative numbers are necessary; so they need not concern us further.

This is a good time to summarize what we have said so far about assigning meaning to the symbols which are to be manipulated by the computer. First, we agreed that the meanings for 64 different 6-bit symbols could be established by a table such as Table 4-1. If we used only these interpretations of symbols in the computer, we would have an unambiguous system which would allow us to represent such abstract concepts as natural-language textual material, arbitrarily large or small numbers, and other special characters, e.g., dollar signs. However, this system makes inefficient use of bits for some purposes (numerical computations, for example), and so we introduced two other ways of interpreting symbols as numbers. Each of these systems has advantages and disadvantages, but by choosing the appropriate one, we can get the advantages of both. Binary notation provides a uniformly spaced set of numbers which makes the most efficient possible use of the bits in the symbol. Wide-range notation greatly increases the size of the largest number and reduces the size of the smallest number which can be represented.

Of course, introducing these other interpretations leads to possible ambiguity in meaning. However, we are familiar in our everyday life with the need to choose the proper interpretation from among all those possible, and the same thing must be done by computer users. In later chapters we shall find that still another interpretation is needed since symbols must also be interpreted as orders to carry out operations, but we shall defer discussion of this interpretation until Chapter 7.

It will not be essential in what follows that we have a detailed knowledge of any of these interpretations of the symbols or that we develop any skill in manipulating the symbols. There are simple algorithms, or rules, available to enable people—or computers—to convert from one number system to another. Anyone who has taken the "new math" courses, or who has children taking them, has been inundated with drills in converting from binary notation to decimal, and vice versa. It is, of course, necessary for some applications that computer users be able to perform such conversions; however, for other applications such facility is not important and for our purposes it is not essential. It is important only to remember that all these interpretations are available and used in various computer applications.

Before concluding the discussion of representations and correspondences between a set of symbols and a set of meanings, we should make some mention of the word *digital*. The word *digital* in the term *digital computer* refers to the fact that our symbols can be used to represent *digits* or *integers,* and, consequently, a computer can process such digits. Already the discussion has shown that this is somewhat of a misnomer since the same symbols can be interpreted with many meanings other than numbers. The term *discrete computer* might be somewhat more appropriate since although the machines make use of many different kinds of devices, the devices all have the characteristic of allowing only a finite, discrete set of conditions and thus produce a finite set of symbols.

Finally, let us mention that a different kind of machine, called an *analog computer,* does make use of devices which can be in an infinite number of different conditions. For example, if smooth wheels were used in an ordinary adding machine, it is intuitively clear that the wheels could stop in an infinite number of arbitrarily close positions rather than in the finite set of discrete positions possible with cogged wheels. There are electric and magnetic devices with similar properties, and analog computers are built using them. Such computers are important because they are useful for certain types of problems, but they are much less versatile, and consequently of much less importance, than digital computers.

To be precise, the devices used in a digital computer can actually be in an infinite number of conditions. To illustrate this, let us reconsider the multiplications performed in Chapter 2. In writing the digits 1, 2, etc., on the blackboard, it is clear that the chalk dust is never placed twice in exactly the same way, and there is really an unlimited set of possible patterns. However, our eye sorts these out and classifies them into 10 discrete classes. Similarly, the binary devices in a digital computer can be in either of two sets of conditions; these sets are quite distinguishable even though each set contains many nearly indistinguishable conditions.

CHAPTER 5

MEMORY

Now that we have a better idea of what sort of symbols are processed in a computer and have a notation for talking about them, we can go on to discuss in more detail the various parts of a computer and how they are organized. In this section we discuss that part of the computer which is called the *memory*. Incidentally, the word *memory* will be used in two ways. First, it sometimes refers to the very simple process (or function) of memory, namely, the retaining of a symbol for an indefinite period of time at the end of which the symbol can be retrieved for use. Second, the word memory sometimes refers to the actual devices in the computer which provide this function. In this chapter we shall discuss some of these devices, but first let us consider how the memory function can be used. Let us go back and reconsider the multiplication which was discussed in Chapter 2 to ascertain just what role was played by the memory (the blackboard) in that example.

The fundamental function of a memory is simply to retain any symbol which is stored there until it is needed at any later time; clearly the blackboard is serving this function, but can we classify some different ways in which it is being used in this problem? Yes, first, we observe that it is being used to store the problem data, that is, the symbols

$$325$$
$$\times\ 47$$
$$\overline{2275}$$
$$1300$$
$$\overline{15275}$$

Figure 5-1   Multiplication using a blackboard.

325 and 47. Second, it stores symbols which represent the intermediate results on lines three and four. Third, it stores the symbols representing the final result. The memory is a vital part of any computer since it must store these three kinds of information in all computer applications. We shall see another very important use for the memory during our discussion of a computer program in Chapter 8. This additional use is presaged in a very rudimentary form by the $\times$ and the underline in our multiplication example.

Before describing the physical devices used for memory, let us consider the principal requirements a memory must meet to function satisfactorily for the preceding three purposes.

First, of course, the memory must be reliable so that any symbol stored there will be available when it is needed later. We must be able to prevent the symbols being erased (changed) by mistake; we can put a "do not erase" sign on the blackboard so that the custodian does not erase the board, but this doesn't work for a computer memory. Second, we must be able to organize the memory into independent locations so that we do not store symbols on top of each other and so that we can retrieve them by simply looking in the right location. A wastebasket can be used to store symbols, but it is a real problem trying to find a particular symbol if you want it later! Third, it is important to be able to store and retrieve symbols rapidly since we do these operations very frequently in all computer applications. Fourth, no matter how much memory is available, there are always problems which need more; therefore, we need large memories. The amount now available depends on the type of device used for the memory; so we shall defer a discussion of size until after the different devices have been described. Fifth, for economic reasons, it is desirable that the memory be reasonably cheap.

It is not difficult to think of many other familiar memory devices which (like the blackboard) have some or all of these characteristics, for example, books, pictures, paper and pencil, or even our own memory.

Historically, one of the earliest landmarks in the development of the computer (cf. page 4) was the *abacus*. An abacus (pictured in Figure 5-2) is nothing more than a memory which is used for storing symbols which represent numbers. Each allowable position of the beads on the rods produces one symbol. When the beads are put in a certain position they stay there indefinitely until the operator changes them—provided that nothing jars the abacus. The operator uses the abacus as a memory device in the same way we used the blackboard in the example in Chapter 2. (For a detailed description of how an abacus is used, see Y. Yoshimo, *The Japanese Abacus Explained.*) Although symbols can be stored and retrieved more rapidly on the abacus than on a blackboard, it is still too slow for modern computers, and, of course, it is very limited in size. What devices are used in a modern computer?

A memory device which is not particularly important but which is very familiar is an ordinary mechanical light switch. Such a switch will stay indefinitely in either of two conditions (which we usually refer to as off and on) so that it can be used as a memory device to store either of two symbols. These switches meet some of the require-

Figure 5-2   Abacus with capacity for storing 11 digits.

ments of a good memory device (for example, they are quite reliable), but they fail badly on the requirement of speed. It probably takes about a half-second to throw the switch from one position to another, and this is not nearly fast enough for modern computers. Consequently, only small numbers, perhaps a hundred, of these switches are used in a typical computer. They are used only in situations where it will be necessary for a person to manually insert some data into the computer memory.

Another simple memory device which has already been mentioned is the punched card. Clearly, a card can be retained for a long period of time, and then it can be examined to see which parts are punched and which are unpunched. Of course, as a memory device, cards are limited because once a hole has been punched, it cannot be unpunched; i.e., the symbol stored in the memory cannot be changed. Punched cards are an important memory device; they will be discussed further in the chapter on input, since they are used mainly in the input process.

By far the most commonly used memory device is a small magnetic ring (also called a magnetic core) which looks like a doughnut less than ⅛ inch in diameter. This ring is made of a ferromagnetic material which can be magnetized in either a clockwise or counterclockwise direction. Thus, like the other devices to which we have referred, it has two distinguishable states. When the ring is magnetized in either direction, it will retain this condition for an indefinite period of time if no attempt is made to switch the direction of magnetization. However, by applying an electric current to a wire which runs through the hole in the doughnut, the direction of magnetization can be changed in less than one millionth of a second. Thus, we see that this device has many of the attributes of an ideal memory device. It is very reliable; it will retain its state for an indefinite time; it can be rapidly changed from one state to the other; and, furthermore, it is reasonably cheap.

Before going further, let's try to clarify what we mean when we say "store a symbol in a memory device." Do you remember our definition of a symbol? A symbol is a device in one specific condition out of a finite set of conditions in which that device can be. Therefore, when we store a symbol in a device, we put the device into the condition corresponding to that symbol. If the device has only two states, or conditions, we have agreed to denote them by the symbols 0 and 1. Thus, to store a 0 in a magnetic ring, we magnetize it in one direction, say clockwise, and to store a 1, we magnetize the ring in a counterclockwise direction. A binary device is said to store a single bit; that is, at any specified time, it is storing the symbol 0 or the symbol 1. To store more than two symbols using binary memory devices, we must use the trick of grouping a number of them in a "super device." For example, if 10 magnetic rings are grouped together and considered as a single device, a 10-bit symbol can be stored in that device, and any one of 1,024 (which is 2^{10}) different symbols can be stored in the device. A collection of binary memory devices grouped in this way is called a *register* or sometimes a *word* of memory; then, a collection of 10 magnetic rings would be referred to as a *10-bit register*.

As mentioned previously, to be useful a memory must be organized into a number of independent locations in each of which a symbol can be stored. In order to identify each word, the memory locations are given *addresses;* that is, they are numbered from 1 to N where N is the number of words in the memory. Thus, by specifying that two symbols be stored in two different locations, we are assured that they will not interfere with or obliterate each other. By retrieving a symbol from a particular location, we are assured of getting the particular symbol we wanted.

Now let us see how groups of magnetic cores can be organized so that large numbers of symbols can be stored at the same time without interfering with one another. The invention in 1947 of a practical way to organize magnetic cores into a memory was one of the important landmarks in the development of the computer (cf. the chart on page 4). As happens so many times, the idea occurred nearly simultaneously to several people, but a basic patent on the scheme has been awarded to J. W. Forrester. The basic organization is very similar to that used by a hotel clerk and is illustrated in Figure 5-3. Suppose the (slightly peculiar) hotel has eight floors with eight rooms on each floor. The message desk may then be arranged as in the figure with eight rows of boxes for each floor with each row containing eight boxes. When asked for a message for room 67, the clerk glances up to the sixth row and across to the seventh box to retrieve any messages there. Notice that the clerk can store or retrieve the message without knowing what the message is as long as he is given the room number.

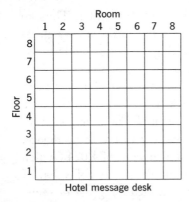 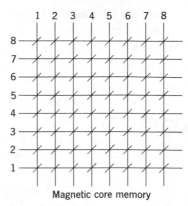

Figure 5-3   Hotel message desk; magnetic core memory.

Similarly, a magnetic core memory having 64 locations would use eight horizontal wires and eight vertical wires with a magnetic core located at each intersection. When storing a symbol in memory location 67, electrical signals are sent along horizontal wire number 6 and vertical wire number 7. The magnetic core at the intersection of these wires is then "set," i.e., put into the proper condition, by the combination of these two signals, but none of the other cores on row 6 or column 7 are disturbed because a single signal is insufficient to change their condition. In order to store a 10-bit symbol, 10 identical arrangements, usually called *planes*, would be stacked on top of each other so that all 10 magnetic cores corresponding to a single location could be set at the same time. To retrieve a symbol from a given location, the same technique is used except that an additional wire must be placed through every core in the plane; the signal which specifies whether the magnetic core was in the 0 or 1 condition appears on this wire. Just like the hotel clerk, the computer can retrieve symbols from a location knowing only the location. There is a slight difference in that only one symbol can be stored at a time in one location of the core memory whereas the clerk can stack many letters in the box.

A picture of part of one plane of cores is shown in Figure 5-4. More than 150,000 of these cores are contained in a memory unit which is 5 inches by 5 inches by 3 inches in size.

Three other devices in common use for memory are also based on magnetic phenomena, in fact, on a technique of recording invented in 1897. They differ mainly in their physical arrangement. The first of these, magnetic tape, is well known in the form of home tape recorders. Exactly the same type of tape is used for computer memory. Each small area of the tape can be either magnetized or unmagnetized; typically across the width of the tape (about ½ inch), seven such spots might be used. Thus, a 7-bit word is located at each position along the tape, and since as many as 800 words can be stored on 1 inch of tape, millions of words can be stored on one reel of tape. The cost per word of tape memory is much less than the corresponding cost for magnetic cores, but the speed with which the symbols can be retrieved is also much less since the tape must be unwound to the location of the desired word. The use of magnetic tape will be discussed further in the chapter on input-output operations.

Another storage device uses magnetic disks which look very much like phonograph records. A bit of information is recorded on these disks in exactly the same fashion as on magnetic tape. A number of these disks, say 10 or 20, are all placed on one spindle. Information can then be written onto, or retrieved from, these disks simultaneously, thus en-

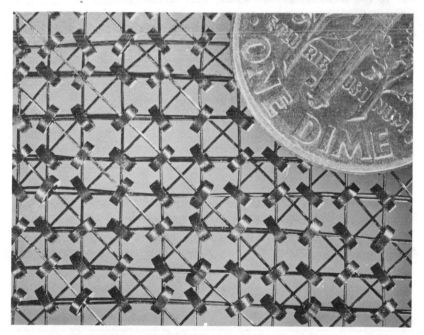

Figure 5-4   Portion of magnetic core memory (courtesy of General Electric Company).

abling faster retrieval than with tape. A third device, which also makes use of magnetic recording, uses a magnetic surface on a cylindrical drum. As this drum rotates, each area of the surface comes under one of a row of reading and writing devices along the drum. At the time that a particular area is under the device, a bit can be either written onto the surface or read off the surface.

The devices discussed above are used for relatively large amounts of memory. In addition, memory devices are needed within the computer for individual bits or single words. It is important that these devices be very fast. They are frequently made of combinations of transistors (much like the ones in your transistor radio) and are called *flip-flops*. The name carries the connotation that the device can be in just two states, i.e., either flipped or flopped.

Since symbols are stored in, or retrieved from, the main memory of a computer very frequently, say 100 million times in a modest-size problem, it is important that this process be very fast. Furthermore, it is necessary to be able to *access*, i.e., store in or retrieve from, any location in the memory. Consequently, it is very desirable that the main memory be *random access*; i.e., any location should be accessible as rapidly as any other. For this reason, magnetic core memories are used as the primary memory for most computers. Magnetic tapes, drums, and disks are at least partially *serial access* since words are read one after another until the desired ones are obtained. This means that the access time for some locations is greater than for others.

The following table summarizes the relative amounts and access times of each kind of memory in a modern large computer.

Memory type	Number of bits	Access time
Cores	10 million	1 millionth of a second
Tape	100 million per reel	Varies: 10 millionths of a second to 10 seconds
Drum	120 million	Varies: 2 millionths to 30 thousandths of a second
Disk	3 billion	Varies: 2 millionths to half a second
Flip-flops	1 thousand	10 billionths of a second
Switches	100	1 second

CHAPTER 6

INPUT-OUTPUT OPERATIONS

An essential requirement for making sensible use of computers is that we be able to put information into the machine and be able to obtain the results in some useful form. During the discussion of the sample problems in Chapter 2, for example, we pointed out that it was necessary to transform spoken words into symbols on a blackboard so that they could be processed. In order to have a useful result of the alphabetizing process, we suggested photographing or copying by hand the list of properly ordered words. In this chapter, we shall be considering those parts of the computer which facilitate such operations.

One of the most frequently used devices for providing input data to a computer is the familiar punched card, and most people are very surprised to find that punched cards were used as long ago as 1780! (We shall discuss this use of cards in Chapter 11.) The first application of punched cards for the representation of large amounts of data was made by Dr. Herman Hollerith in 1890. Hollerith was an official of the U.S. Census Bureau who realized that unless some means of speeding up the analysis of census data were found, the analysis could not be completed in the 10 years between censuses. He recognized the value of punched cards for this purpose, devised a code for representing data on the cards, and invented the necessary machines to meet his needs. Incidentally, he went on to found a company to produce these machines, and this company later (1924) became the International Business Machines Corporation. Since IBM makes and sells about 75 percent of the world's computers, he obviously had a significant impact on the development of computers. Let's see how punched cards are used for the input of information to a computer.

The use of punched cards actually requires two separate pieces of equipment. The first is called a *key punch*, looks somewhat like a large typewriter, and is not physically connected to the computer in any way. When a typist presses a key which is labeled with a *character*, i.e., a letter, number, or some special character (such as those in Table 4-1), the machine punches a number of holes in one column of the card. Each column of the card has 12 areas in which holes may be punched. Thus, in effect, the character is changed into a 12-bit word which we would represent by writing the holes as 1 and the unpunched areas as 0. Most cards have 80 columns so that no more than 80 characters can be punched on one card. One of the more commonly used representations, or correspondences between characters and punches, is shown in Figure 6-1.

Each of the digits and letters is represented by the particular pattern of punches in the column beneath the corresponding printed character at the top of the card. Although computer users can learn to read the patterns of holes, it is much easier to have the punch print the

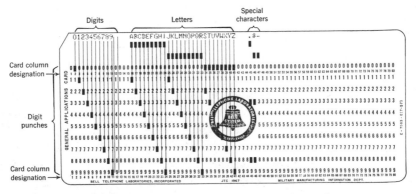

Figure 6-1   Correspondence between characters and punches.

characters at the top of the card at the same time it punches the holes. We then have the best of both worlds—the computer can read the holes easily, and the computer user can read the printed characters!

Once the information has been converted into holes in the cards, it is ready for another piece of equipment called a *card reader*. This piece of equipment is actually attached to the computer by a set of wires. A stack of cards is placed in the card reader, and these cards are then examined one at a time within the reader. By passing the card under a number of metal brushes or contacts, the holes are converted into short electrical signals. These signals are used to transmit the symbol from the card reader to the computer; usually the symbols are stored directly in the computer memory. Note that the card reader makes no use of any of the printed characters on the card. These are there solely to help the computer user interpret the card if necessary.

We have referred several times to the "transmission" of symbols, and perhaps we should clarify this idea. Since a symbol is something physical —a device in some particular condition—one way to transmit symbols would be to actually move the device from one location to another. In a few cases this is done; for example, we might pick up a deck of punched cards and physically move them from one machine to another. However, the ability to transmit a symbol from one location to another in less than a millionth of a second is essential to obtain high processing speed; consequently, there is not time for much mechanical motion. To get this high speed, symbols are usually first transformed into electrical signals; these electrical signals are then transmitted at very high speeds to the desired location; and then the electrical signals may be transformed into some other form. For example, a magnetic core which is magnetized in a clockwise direction can be used to generate a pulse of electric current which can travel 1,000 feet in a millionth of a second and then cause another magnetic core at that point to be magnetized in a clockwise direction. Thus, strictly speaking, the transmission of a symbol involves causing a symbol at one location to generate a corresponding symbol at another point. Since in our notation all symbols are represented just by 0s and 1s, we can represent the new corresponding symbol in exactly the same way as the old. Thus, we can ignore the fact that the physical device was not moved and just think of this process as moving the symbol from one location to the other.

It should be quite clear that it is desirable that the input process be carried out very rapidly. It is possible to add two numbers in a few millionths of a second; clearly, we could not make good use of this speed if it took us as much time to put these numbers in the computer as it takes to type them. Although the key punch is operated by a person at manual speeds, once prepared, a stack of these cards (usually called a *deck*) can be read into the machine's memory at the much faster rate of about 500 cards per minute; this corresponds to a maximum rate of about 40,000 symbols per minute. However, this is still not fast enough for the economical use of some computers.

In order to obtain still higher speeds, magnetic tape is frequently used as an intermediate input medium. We have already referred to the use of reels of magnetic tape as a memory device for storing symbols. In order to use it as an input mechanism, it is necessary to use a special piece of equipment which converts the input information to the corresponding magnetic symbol on the tape. (This is frequently done by first punching this information onto cards and then transforming the information from card punches to magnetic symbols by using a card reader.) After this has been done, the reel of tape is mounted on a tape unit which is connected by wires to the computer. As the tape unwinds, the magnetic bits are converted into electrical signals; these are transmitted to the computer, and the symbols are stored in the computer memory one word at a time. This process can take place at a speed of about 80,000 characters per second, which is about 120 times as fast as characters can be read from cards.

After the data processing, some form of output device is essential. Frequently, the results of the processing are going to be used at a later time for additional processing; in this case it is desirable that the results be produced in a form which is suitable for computer input. Consequently, a card punch is frequently attached to the computer so that electrical signals corresponding to a particular symbol operate a key which punches holes in a card which correspond precisely to that symbol. After all the symbols for one card are punched, another card moves into position, and the next set of electrical signals operate keys to punch this card. At the end of this operation, a deck of punched cards has been produced just as though characters had been typed on a key punch; this deck can be used later as input to another computer operation. This punching operation can take place at a rate of about 250 cards per minute.

Since this operation is relatively slow and since it may be necessary to store millions of symbols which would require a large volume of cards, magnetic tape is frequently used instead of punched cards for intermediate output. Electrical signals corresponding to the output symbol are transformed into a magnetic symbol on the tape, and consecutive symbols are placed in consecutive positions on the tape as the tape is unwound. After the tape is rewound, it is ready to serve as input to the computer later on. This process can take place at a rate of about 80,000 characters per second, and a single reel of tape less than a foot in diameter can hold symbols which would require 250,000 cards.

However, it is always necessary at some point to get output which can be used or interpreted by people. The most common way of doing this is by using a *printer*. This machine operates much like a typewriter except that it usually prints an entire line of type at one time. An output symbol is converted into electrical signals which are transmitted to the printer; there are many different ways in which these signals may be converted into print. One way is to have these signals operate a magnet which presses a key corresponding to this symbol against a roll of paper. The character on the key is thus printed so that the output operation has resulted in the printing of either a letter or a number or some special character. Note that this means that the printer assumes a particular representation or correspondence between the output symbols and the alphanumeric characters. If the output is to make sense, it is necessary that this correspondence be the same one used within the computer to interpret these symbols. For example, if the output symbol has 6 bits, the correspondence of Table 4-1 might be used; this would allow the printer to print uppercase English letters, the 10 digits, a blank, a comma, a period, a dollar sign, etc. Naturally, it is more expensive to provide for more characters. Consequently, it has been very common to use 6-bit output symbols (which would provide for a maximum of 64 characters) with from 40 to 60 of these actually being used. It appears likely that 7-bit output symbols will become common in the near future; the larger number of characters possible will then commonly include lowercase English letters as well as more special characters.

Ø   00030   00000 0 15200

```
                        665            END     FINE              20326650
                        666   FINE     ØPBITS  400000            20326660
                        667   NAME     MACRØ                     20326670
                        668   NAME     INSTR                     20326680
                        669   NAME     MACRØ                     20326690
                        670   INST     INST                      20326700
                        671            END                       20326710
                        672   INST     MACRØ   CR1,CR2,CR3,CR4   20326720
                        673   UNIT     SET1    0                 20326730
                        674            LØCTR   CR1,CR2           20326740
                        675   CR3      SET     *-1               20326750
                        676            USE     A                 20326760
                        677            PZE     CR1               20326770
                        678            USE     B                 20326780
                        679            TSX     CR2,4             20326790
                        680            USE     C                 20326800
                        681            PZE     CR3,1             20326810
                        682            USE     I                 20326820
                        683            PZE                       20326830
                        684            USE     H                 20326840
                        685   CR4      SET     *-1               20326850
                        686            USE     G                 20326860
                        687            PZE     CR4,1             20326870
                        688            USE     E                 20326880
                        689            SXA     X12,1             20326890
                        690            SXD     X12,2             20326900
                        691            SXD     TMP1,4            20326910
                        692   INSNØ    SET     INSNØ+1           20326920
                        693            NUMB    (1,2,3,4,5,6,7,8,9,10,11,12,13,14,15,16,17,18,19,20,$  20326930
                        694            ETC     21,22,23,24,25,26,27,28,29,30)  20326940
                        695            END                       20326950
                        696   NUMB     MACRØ                     20326960
                        697            IRP     L                 20326970
                        698            IFF     L-INSNØ,1         20326980
                        699            LABEL   (INSTRUMENT),L    20326990
                        700            IF                        20327000
                        701            GØ                        20327010
                        702            IRP                       20327020
```

Figure 6-2   Sample printer output.

In order to print words and multidigit numbers, the printer must be able to print a number of characters on the same line. To accomplish this, the printer assumes that consecutive output characters, including blanks, are to be printed side by side on the same line until a special control character, which acts like a typewriter carriage return, is received. Upon recognition of this control character, the printer moves the paper an amount determined by the control character so that variable spacing between lines is possible and then begins printing the next line. Thus, in addition to the characters to be printed, the printer must be supplied with the proper control characters to specify movement of the paper at the appropriate points.

Since it would be very wasteful to let expensive, high-speed computers spend very much time typing out results and since there is a great deal of printing to be done, printers are made to go at extremely high speeds. Some can type as fast as 1,200 lines per minute with 120 to 150 characters per line. A sample of the output obtained from a printer is shown in Figure 6-2.

Although printed output is suitable for some applications, graphic output is more useful for many others. For example, originally, if a computer were being used to calculate the amount of weekly sales of some brand of soap, the results would be printed out as 52 numbers, and then quite frequently a clerk would be asked to plot these numbers on a graph so that it would be possible for a manager to see how the sales were changing. Now output devices are available which produce the graph directly rather than printing numbers which must be manually converted to a graph. One such device is called a *microfilm printer*. It makes use of a tube which is something like a television screen. The output symbols from the computer are converted into electrical signals which are displayed on the face of the tube as lines or letters or numbers. A picture is taken of the tube face using a 35-mm camera, and this film is then processed using conventional photographic processes so that the output can be seen through a microfilm viewer or an enlargement made if desirable. Such an output device has even been used to produce movies under the direction of a computer. A sample of the output produced by this device is shown in Figure 6-3.

Although we have not exhausted the subject of input-output equipment by any means, the role which it plays in the operation of

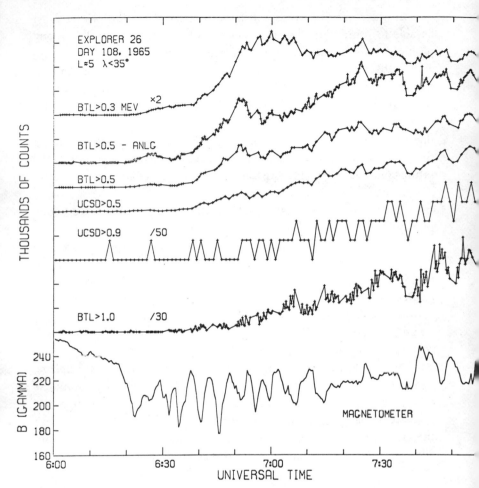

Figure 6-3   Sample of computer output produced on microfilm printer.

the computer should be clear. In many respects, these parts of the computer seem rather simple, probably because they are not too unfamiliar. We are accustomed to punched cards, typewriters, and even magnetic tape, and they may seem unimportant to some of the startling applications of computers about which we've heard. However, the input-output operations often turn out to be the key to the successful application of computers. Consequently, a great deal of effort by computer manufacturers is going into the attempt to simplify input and to produce output in a variety of readily useful forms. We shall defer discussion of some of this work until later, but, as an example, we shall mention some input devices which were developed to extend the application of computers to banking. The strange-looking figures appearing at the bottom of most checks in the last few years were put there so that computers could be used in sorting these checks. A special input device was developed to simplify the transformation of some of the information from the check to the computer. There are actually two types of devices in use of which one is optical and the other magnetic. They both recognize only certain types of characters, which is the reason that the figures at the bottom of the check look so strange. However, the information contained in these figures requires no manual operations, such as key punching, to make it accessible to a computer.

CHAPTER 7

SYMBOL-PROCESSING OPERATIONS

At this point in our study of computers we have found out what the symbols that are being processed are, how they are interpreted, how to get them in and out of the computer, and how they can be stored until we want to make use of them. Now we are ready to consider how these symbols can be manipulated in useful ways. As was indicated in Chapter 2, these operations are carried out in that portion of the computer called the processor.

By considering some examples of problems suitable for computers, we can easily recognize some desirable symbol-processing operations. The multiplication example discussed in Chapter 2 brought out the necessity for having *arithmetic operations*; that is, when we are interpreting the symbols as numbers, we would like to be able to combine two symbols and obtain a third, which corresponds to the result of adding, subtracting, multiplying, or dividing them. Many people think these are the only types of operations carried out in the computer, but there are many more. The arithmetic operations will be described in more detail a little later, but let us consider another example to illustrate the need for other operations.

Suppose that the board of education asks the principal of the local high school whether all his students are either residents of the town or are paying out-of-town tuition. If this is a very progressive, up-to-date principal, he probably has a great deal of information on file for each student. Let us assume that he has, in fact, all this information stored on one punched card for each student. Further, let us assume that the principal was foresighted enough to use one column of the card to record whether or not the student was a resident of the town and another column to record whether or not the student was paying tuition. A secretary could then check each card to determine whether at least one of these columns indicated yes; if so, the card could be put in one box, and if neither column is marked yes, the card could be put in another box. If all the cards go in the first box, the principal can report that all the students are either residents or are paying tuition; if there are any cards in the second box, he'd better try to collect some tuition.

What kind of operations were involved here? Clearly, there was no adding, subtracting, multiplying, or dividing; instead, the operations involved are representative of a class called the *logical operations*. For example, the secretary had to determine for each card whether an entry in *either* the first column *or* the second column was yes. This procedure corresponds to the INCLUSIVE OR operation, which is defined by the following table:

INCLUSIVE OR

Symbol A	Symbol B	Output symbol
0	0	0
0	1	1
1	0	1
1	1	1

The table can be summarized by saying that the output symbol is 1 if symbol A *or* symbol B is 1, *or* both symbols are 1; otherwise, the output symbol is 0. The correspondence between the secretary's procedure and this operation is seen by assuming that symbols A and B are the words in the columns and that a no in a card column is represented by a 0 and a yes by a 1. Then a 1 for the result of the operation corresponds to the secretary's putting the card in the first box, and a 0 corresponds to putting the card in the second box. Consequently, if the principal's secretary were busy with other things and if there were a computer available which could carry out the INCLUSIVE OR operation, the computer could read in the information punched on the cards and make the proper determination for each card.

But now what about drawing the conclusion requested by the board of education? How can the computer determine whether *all* students are either residents or are paying tuition? This can be done by using another logical operation called the AND operation which is defined by the following table.

AND

Symbol A	Symbol B	Output symbol
0	0	0
0	1	0
1	0	0
1	1	1

This table can be summarized by saying that the output symbol is 1 if both symbol A *and* symbol B are 1, and 0 otherwise. If the computer has stored the result of performing the INCLUSIVE OR operation for each card, it can determine whether that result for the first card *and* for the second card *and* for the third card, etc., is 1. If so, the result of applying all these AND operations is 1; otherwise the result is 0. If the computer prints out 1, the principal knows everything is all right; if the computer prints out 0, the principal knows some student is neither a resident nor one paying tuition.

There are several other logical operations which are quite useful and frequently provided in computers. Two of these are defined by the following tables:

EXCLUSIVE OR

Symbol A	Symbol B	Output symbol
0	0	0
0	1	1
1	0	1
1	1	0

NOT

Symbol A	Output symbol
0	1
1	0

The EXCLUSIVE OR can be summarized by saying that the output symbol is 1 if either one *or* the other, but not both, of the input symbols A and B is 1. The NOT operation involves only one input symbol, and the output symbol is 1 if the input is *not* 1, and 0 otherwise.

These operations can be defined for multibit symbols by carrying out the same operations on each bit of the symbol. The following examples for each operation should make this definition clear.

	AND	INCLUSIVE OR	EXCLUSIVE OR	NOT
Symbol A	001110	001110	001110	001110
Symbol B	101010	101010	101010	
Output symbol	001010	101110	100100	110001

We already have a respectable list of operations to provide; let's consider a little more carefully just how they can be carried out. We said at the beginning of this chapter that all of these operations are carried out in some equipment, or electrical circuits, called the processor. The processor actually consists of a group of circuits, one circuit for each operation. Our picture of the processor is thus a group of separate circuits such as is indicated in Figure 7-1.

In order to carry out a particular operation, the input symbols must be transmitted to the proper circuit, the operation performed, and then the output symbol must be stored someplace in the computer. Frequently, one or more of the symbols to be processed must be obtained from the memory, and many times the output symbol is stored there. If wires were provided to transmit symbols from each of the circuits in the processor to each location in the memory, millions of wires would be required. This is exactly the same problem faced by the telephone company in providing for calls between any pair of telephones in the country, and computer designers solve it in the same way as the telephone company. A switch is located at the processor so that any one of the circuits can be connected to a wire which can transmit symbols to the memory; this wire is an example of the wires referred to in Chapter 2 as *data links* or *data busses*. At the memory this wire is connected to another switch which can direct the symbol to any

Processor

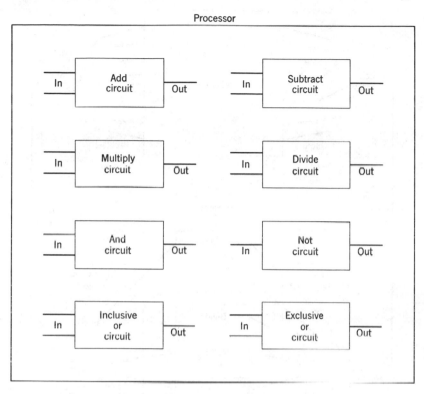

Figure 7-1   Block diagram of processor.

memory location. A similar arrangement is used to bring symbols from the memory to the processor. We now have the somewhat more detailed picture of the computer shown in Figure 7-2. Note that fewer wires are required because of the use of the switches.

As you may have guessed, it is not only necessary to provide a specific circuit for each operation, there also must be separate circuits to carry out the same operation for different representations. For example, if a machine represents numbers in both binary notation and wide-range notation, there must be an adder corresponding to each type of representation. To see the type of trouble which arises otherwise, consider the result of using a circuit which produces a symbol corresponding to the result of adding two numbers in binary notation

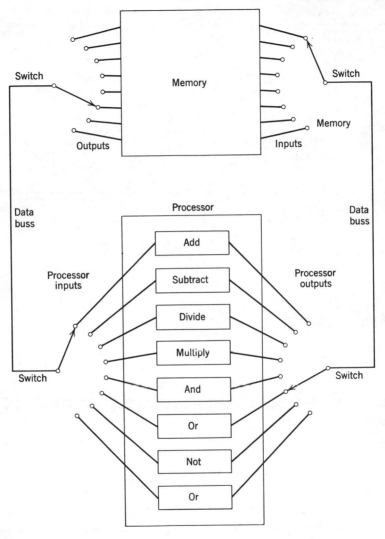

Figure 7-2   Diagram of connections between processor and memory.

when the input symbols actually represent numbers in wide-range notation. If the input symbols are

100001000000111 (which represents 14 in wide-range notation and
16,903 in binary notation) and

000001000000010 (which represents 1 in wide-range notation and 514 in binary notation)

the output symbol of a binary-adder circuit would be 100010000001001. This represents 17,417 in binary notation and would be the correct answer if the input symbols had that interpretation; however, it represents 36 in wide-range notation and, thus, is not the right answer, which is 15. In making use of any operation, such as addition, which may be used with symbols corresponding to two or more representations, it is up to the person using the computer to make sure that he specifies that the circuit be used which corresponds to the proper interpretation of the symbols. If the wrong circuit is used, the computer will go blithely ahead, but the results will be nonsense. We shall see how the user specifies the proper circuit in the next chapter.

Although it is not the purpose of this book to teach computer design, we do wish to say something about how the individual circuits for carrying out specific operations are built. The first person to build a physical machine to carry out some of these operations was a Frenchman, Blaise Pascal. He used a gear-driven mechanism which is closely related to present-day mechanical adding machines. It was capable of addition and subtraction and used a decimal representation of numbers. As indicated on the chart (page 4), a great many people developed other mechanisms for carrying out these operations as well as multiplication and division. One of the most important of these was Charles Babbage. He not only proposed ways of carrying out these operations but envisioned combining them with memory devices and an output printer to obtain a computer remarkably like those produced now. Babbage successfully designed and built a machine to do addition and print the results, but the technology of the times was just not adequate to build his entire machine out of the complicated assemblage of gears and levers he designed. Although he was an extremely ingenious man —inventor, machinist, engineer, mathematician, printer, and politician (since he needed to get support from the English government)—Babbage never got his complete "analytical engine" going.

Just before and during World War II, G. R. Stibitz and S. B. Williams built circuits using relays, electromechanical devices, to do the arithmetic operations. This was the first attempt to build computers with other than exclusively mechanical devices. However, it was not until the late 1940s and early 1950s when computer designers began to use electronic devices—first vacuum tubes and then transistors—that the "computer revolution" really got underway. Modern high-speed computers use somewhat different circuits for each operation, but they are all made of *solid-state devices,* i.e., transistors and diodes. These devices are cheap and very fast, but even more importantly, they are reliable. Since large machines contain many hundreds of thousands of components—any one of which can cause the machine to fail—it would be impossible to achieve reliable operation for machines of this complexity if gears, relays, or vacuum tubes were the major components. However, the reliability of solid-state devices is high enough so that bigger and bigger machines are being built. Figure 7-3 is a picture of an installation which is now using computers representative of three different stages in computer development. The earliest of these (IBM 705) uses mainly vacuum tube circuits, the second (IBM 7074) uses mainly transistor circuits, and the most recent (IBM 360/65) uses newer microminiaturized solid-state circuits. The processing speed of the latest is 400 times that of the earliest.

We shall not attempt here to discuss the engineering design of these circuits, but we can give a simple picture of their operation. These circuits make use of devices called *logic gates* as well as the memory devices called flip-flops to which we referred earlier. One type of logic gate called an AND gate has two input wires and one output wire, and has the characteristic that it produces an output whenever both inputs are present, but it will not produce an output otherwise. In other words, the gate is constructed so that one input alone is not strong enough to push through to the output, but two inputs together are strong enough to push through and cause a signal at the output. A simple way to think of such a device is to compare it with a threshold which is, say, the height of a kitchen shelf. Two small boys cannot reach the cookie jar by themselves, but if they are both present at the same time, one can lift the other over the threshold and, thus, produce an output. This is almost exactly what happens in an AND gate constructed out of transistors, magnetic cores, tunnel diodes, or other kinds of exotic devices. If the threshold, i.e., the shelf, is lowered, an output is produced when either one *or* the other boy is present; an electronic

Figure 7-3 *Three generations of computers in use at Aetna Life and Casualty, Hartford, Connecticut.*

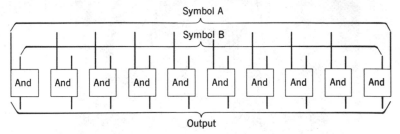

Figure 7-4   Circuit for carrying out logical AND operation.

OR gate operates in analogous fashion. A third type of device, called a NOT gate, might be pictured as a storekeeper who displays cookies when there are no little boys present but puts them out of sight as soon as a boy shows up.

It should be fairly clear that these gates can be used to construct the circuits required for carrying out the logical operations. For example, to build a circuit which carries out the logical AND operation on a 10-bit word, the designer connects 10 AND gates as shown in Figure 7-4.

Somewhat surprisingly, it turns out that using only flip-flops and these three types of logic gates, circuits can be constructed for doing all of the other operations which we have mentioned. Figure 7-5 shows how such devices can be used to build a *binary adder,* i.e., a circuit whose output symbol corresponds to the result of adding two numbers represented in binary notation by the input symbols.

Although a separate circuit is required to carry out every operation

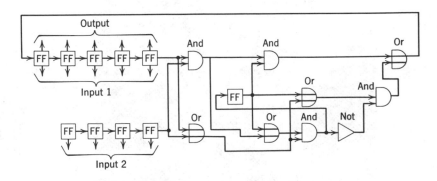

Figure 7-5   Circuit diagram for binary adder.

which the machine can be instructed to do, computer designers are very clever in finding ways to use parts of these circuits in more than one operation. In fact, much of the effort involved in a computer design goes into finding ways to reduce the cost of the computer by making as much multiple use as possible of circuits for different operations. All of these operations are carried out very rapidly in a modern machine. The logical operations and additions typically require on the order of a millionth of a second, and divisions, which are usually the slowest operation, are done in less than a thousandth of a second.

In order to design the circuits used to carry out the operations which he is going to provide in a computer, the designer must first specify what interpretation of symbols he will use. Then he chooses an *algorithm,* or particular sequence of steps, for carrying out each opera tion. Finally, he finds a way of interconnecting logic gates and flip-flops to carry out these steps. The analysis required in this last step frequently makes use of *Boolean algebra,* which is a type of mathematics specifically suited to the use of just two values or numbers. We cannot describe this algebra here, but it should not seem surprising that such an algebra should be well suited to the design of circuits which are built of binary devices.

Incidentally, it may seem surprising that it is necessary to choose an algorithm for such operations as multiplication or division. Is there more than one way to do them? The answer is yes; in fact, there are many different ways of doing any of these operations. The designer makes his choice among them so as to maximize the speed and to minimize the amount of equipment required for the circuit.

CHAPTER 8

THE CONTROL PROCESS

The three functions—memory, processing, and input-output—discussed in the last three chapters were all important parts of the solutions of the two sample problems discussed in Chapter 2. However, we recall that in the analysis of the steps in their solutions, we recognized that doing these steps in a correct order was also vital to obtaining a correct solution. In this chapter we shall consider how this process of ordering, or *controlling*, the sequential steps in the solution of a problem on a computer is carried out.

In order to control the sequence of operations going on in a computer, the very first requirement is that it must be possible to give an order to carry out particular operations. These orders to carry out operations are called *instructions* (or sometimes *orders*), and the entire set of such orders for a particular computer is referred to as the *instruction set* or *order code* for that computer. Let us begin the discussion of control by considering the form of these instructions.

From the description given in the last chapter of the operations carried out by the processor, it is clear that for these operations the corresponding instructions should specify the location of the input symbols and the location where the result of the operation is to be stored. Consequently, instructions for operations which use two input symbols (e.g., the addition of two numbers) would need to specify an operation and three addresses or locations. Such an instruction set is referred to as a *three-address instruction set*.

To simplify the instructions, it is customary in most computers to reduce the number of locations from which input symbols can be retrieved and/or to reduce the number of locations in which the output symbol can be placed. For example, a special memory register (frequently called the *accumulator*) can be made part of the processor and used in such manner that most operations obtain one of their input symbols from this register and also store their output symbol in that register. By this means, it is possible to use instructions which need to specify only one location or address in addition to the operation; such an instruction set is called a *single-address instruction set*.

To illustrate these ideas, let us detail part of the instruction set for a hypothetical computer which we shall call the THC 1 computer. We shall assume that the THC 1 uses both binary notation and wide-range notation for numbers; that it has 1,024 words of memory, each memory word has 15 bits; and that it uses single-address instructions which make use of a 15-bit accumulator register. We shall fix other characteristics of our hypothetical machine as necessary.

Naturally, in the THC 1 just as in real computers, we shall need operations for processing, input-output, memory, and control purposes. For each of these operations we shall need an instruction to direct that the operation be carried out. We shall consider these four classes of operations, and the corresponding instructions, in the above order.

To get started, let us define the arithmetic operations for numbers in binary notation. The instruction BINADD N (the N is replaced by a number in an actual instruction) directs the following operation: The binary number in memory location N is added to the binary number in the accumulator, and the resulting binary number is stored in the accumulator. For example, suppose the accumulator contains a binary 3 and memory location 7 contains a binary 2, then after the instruction BINADD 7 is carried out, the accumulator contains a binary 5 (see Figure 8-1). In this instruction the BINADD is referred to as the *operation part* and the N as the *address part* of the instruction.

The instructions BINSUB N, BINMUL N, and BINDIV N are all carried out similarly with the results being stored in the accumulator and the subtrahend, multiplier, and divisor retrieved from memory location N. It is very important that we understand the role of the address part of these instructions. Looking back to the example in Figure 8-1, we see that the address was 7, but the number stored in that memory location was 2, not 7. The number given in the address part of the instruction is not the number to be added (or subtracted, multiplied, divided); instead, it specifies the memory location where that number is to be obtained.

Since we have another type of number representation, namely wide-range notation, we must have similar instructions available to manipulate numbers in this representation. Thus, the instruction WRADD N is interpreted by the computer in exactly the same fashion except that a different circuit in the processor is used to carry out the processing. We might call this particular circuit the WR adder. Similar circuits must be available for WRSUB N, WRMUL N, WRDIV N. Of course, it would be nice if the machine would not need to be told which representation was to be used and would automatically choose the right circuit. However, usually it has no way of doing this, and so it is up to the person using the computer to make sure that he uses the instruction which corresponds to the proper interpretation of the symbols. If he uses the wrong one, the computer will go blithely ahead, but the results will be incorrect (see example in Chapter 7).

Although these four operations are the only ones necessary for carrying out arithmetic calculations, most computers have many other related operations which simplify and speed up arithmetic. However, they really involve no new basic ideas, and so we shall not provide for them in the THC 1. However, we do need some of the basic logical operations for processing symbols which were described in Chapter 7. Let us define the instructions for these.

	Before BINADD 7	After BINADD 7
Memory location 7	000000000000010	000000000000010
Accumulator	000000000000011	000000000000101

Figure 8-1 Illustration of the operation BINADD 7.

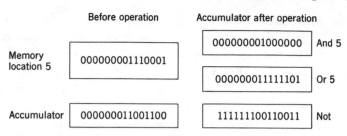

Figure 8-2   Illustrations of logical operations.

The instructions OR *N* and AND *N* direct that the symbols in memory location *N* and the accumulator are to be combined according to the OR and AND operations (defined in Chapter 7), and the resulting symbol is to be stored in the accumulator. The instruction NOT (notice that it uses no address portion) directs that the operation NOT should be applied to the symbol in the accumulator. Examples of each of these are given in Figure 8-2 by showing the symbol which results in the accumulator after any one of these operations is ordered.

We now have a total of 11 processing operations, 8 arithmetic and 3 logical, and this will be sufficient for the THC 1. Next, let us describe the two instructions that direct our hypothetical computer to carry out input and output operations. We shall assume that there is just one input device (a card reader), and so the THC 1 carries out the instruction READ *N* by taking the binary symbol which appears at the terminals of the card reader and by storing it in memory location *N*. For example, READ 5 means take the symbol appearing at the input and store it in memory location 5. *Note that the symbol being stored is probably not a 5.*

Similarly, we assume that there is a single output device, a printer, and the THC 1 carries out the instruction WRITE *N* by obtaining the symbol stored in memory location *N* and by printing the corresponding characters. As was discussed in the chapter on input-output devices, the printer must assume a particular correspondence between the output symbols and the characters it prints. We shall use the basic correspondence shown in Table 4-1, which specifies characters for 6-bit symbols. Since the memory words are 15 bits long, the right-hand 12 bits specify the printing of two consecutive characters and the other 3 bits can be ignored. We shall assume that one of the 6-bit symbols causes the printer to move the paper by the width of a line of printing, but since we won't require this amount of detail in the following, we shall not bother to specify the printer any further. For example, WRITE 7 transmits the right-hand 12 bits of the word in memory location 7 to the printer and prints the two appropriate characters.

Next, we shall need some instructions to facilitate using the memory. The instruction STORE N directs the THC 1 to transmit the symbol located in the accumulator to the memory and store it in location N. The instruction FETCH N directs the computer to obtain the symbol from location N in the memory and store it in the accumulator.

As we discuss the control process further, we shall find that a few more instructions are necessary, but for the present this is enough. Notice that although we have provided no specific instruction for simply transmitting a symbol from one place to another, the operations we have discussed typically involve obtaining one or more symbols from some location, transmitting them to a processor, doing the processing, and transmitting the resulting symbol to some other location. In many cases, the name of the operation does not explicitly indicate that transmission is taking place, but it is implied.

Now that we have a means of giving orders to the THC 1, we are ready to make use of our computer. However, when we give an instruction to, say, BINADD 7 (that is, use the binary adder to add the number in memory location 7 to the number now in the accumulator), there must be a circuit which gets the symbol from the memory, sees that it is transmitted to the binary adder, connects the accumulator to the binary adder, and instructs the binary adder to start operation.

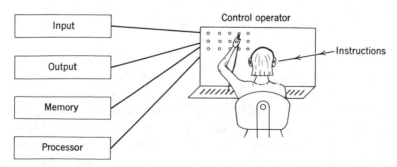

Figure 8-3   The control unit is analogous to a telephone operator.

This piece of equipment is called the *control unit*. It performs many of the roles of a telephone operator. It has data links for transmitting symbols between all parts of the computer. After being given an instruction, the "operator" decides which circuits are to be used and connects switches (such as those shown in Figure 7-2) to establish the proper paths. The operator then sends signals ("rings the phones") to start the symbol transmission and the processing operation. After checking that the instruction has been performed, the operator disconnects the switches and starts in on the next instruction.

Since the operator is actually a circuit similar to all the others in the computer, it must receive its instructions as symbols just like those used to represent letters and numbers. Consequently, another correspondence must be set up between these symbols and all the instructions which the control unit is to be able to recognize. Ordinarily, only one such correspondence is used within a particular computer; that is, one instruction is always represented by just one symbol in the machine. Notice that this differs from the case for letters and numbers for which several correspondences are likely to be used in a single machine.

Let us set up a correspondence for the instructions of our computer. Since we shall require no more than 32 instructions, 5 bits will be enough to allow a unique symbol for the operation part of each instruction. Since the THC 1 has 1,024 memory locations, we shall need a 10-bit binary number ($2^{10}=1,024$) to refer to these locations. Consequently, our instructions will consist of a 5-bit operation part and a 10-bit address part. Table 8-1 shows one possible correspondence for the instructions with the first 5 bits representing the operation part.

The last five instructions in this table will be discussed shortly, but they are included here so that we shall have all the instructions conveniently listed in a single table. In an instruction, the Xs represent positions in the address portion of the instruction which are replaced by either 0 or 1 in order to specify the proper address. For example, the instruction BINADD 7 corresponds to the symbol 11001000000111, and WRSUB 35 is represented by 100100000100011.

A block diagram of the computer we have specified up to this point is shown in Figure 8-4. It is essentially a complete, although slightly simplified, picture of early "programmable" digital computers. In fact Charles Babbage, although unable to complete the construction of his

Table 8-1 Instructions for THC 1 computer

BINADD	N	11001XXXXXXXXXX
BINSUB	N	11010XXXXXXXXXX
BINMUL	N	11011XXXXXXXXXX
BINDIV	N	11100XXXXXXXXXX
WRADD	N	10001XXXXXXXXXX
WRSUB	N	10010XXXXXXXXXX
WRMUL	N	10011XXXXXXXXXX
WRDIV	N	10100XXXXXXXXXX
AND	N	00001XXXXXXXXXX
OR	N	00010XXXXXXXXXX
NOT		00011000000000000
READ	N	01001XXXXXXXXXX
WRITE	N	01010XXXXXXXXXX
STORE	N	01011XXXXXXXXXX
FETCH	N	01100XXXXXXXXXX
GOTO	N	01101XXXXXXXXXX
CZGOTO	N	01110XXXXXXXXXX
CLEAR		01111000000000000
HALT		11111000000000000
LZGOTO	N	11110XXXXXXXXXX

machine, clearly envisaged almost exactly this basic structure as early as 1830. In order to operate it, a sequence of instructions, called the *program,* is fed into the control unit. The particular part of the control unit which receives the symbols representing the instructions and starts the necessary control operation is called the *instruction decoder.* The instructions could be fed into the instruction decoder by punching the corresponding symbols on cards and by using the same sort of card reader as is used for supplying input symbols to the computer memory. These instructions are then carried out one at a time in exactly the order they are presented in the program.

Table 8-2 Program for reading two numbers, adding, and storing the result

Instruction	Explanation
010010000000000	Read number into location zero
010010000000001	Read number into location 1
110010000000000	Add number in location zero into accumulator
110010000000001	Add number in location 1 into accumulator
010110000000010	Store sum in location 2

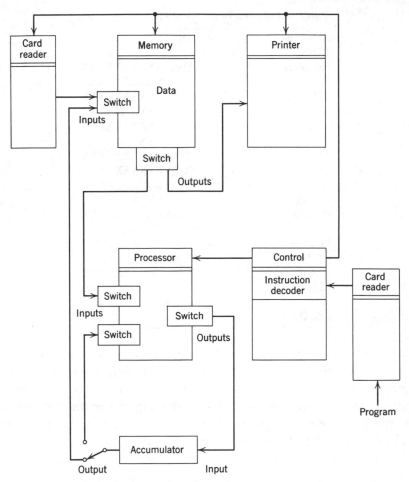

Figure 8-4   *Block diagram of early computers.*

The process of preparing a suitable sequence of instructions to do a desired job is called *programming the computer*. We shall be discussing this very important phase of computer use in a later chapter, but right now let's see what a simple program looks like. For example, here is the program which would be written to read in two numbers, add them, and store the result.

Now let's see how this program could control the action of the THC 1 so as to perform the desired function. We shall assume that the five instructions have been punched on cards and that the cards are mounted in a card reader attached to the control unit of the computer. In addition, the two numbers to be added have been punched on cards, and the cards are mounted in the input card reader of the THC 1. When the *start* button of the THC 1 is pushed, the control unit sends a signal to its card reader which directs the reading of the instruction on the first card. This symbol is transmitted to the instruction decoder in the control unit. The instruction decoder determines that this is a read instruction and sends a signal to the input card reader directing that the first card be read, and also sets the memory switch so that this symbol is stored in memory location zero.

After this process is complete, the control unit sends a signal to its card reader directing that the next instruction be read. This instruction is carried out just like the first except that the memory switch is set to store the symbol in location 1.

Again, the control unit directs that the next instruction be read. After determining that this is an add instruction, the decoder sets switches so that the number in memory location zero and the number in the accumulator are both transmitted to the binary add circuit. It then sends a signal to that circuit directing it to start the add operation (which ends, you remember, with the result of the addition stored in the accumulator).

After this operation is complete, the control unit directs that the next instruction be read. This operation is carried out just like the preceding except that one of the numbers is obtained from memory location 1.

The next instruction is then read and found to be a store operation. The control unit sets the necessary switches so that the number in the accumulator can be transmitted to memory location 2.

After this operation is complete, the control unit directs that the next instruction be read, but it finds that there are no more cards to be read. If this lack of further cards is interpreted as an instruction to halt the machine, the machine could stop operation. However, it is safer to have a positive instruction to do this, and a special HALT instruction was included in Table 8-1 for just this purpose. For safer operation, this instruction should be included as the sixth and last instruction of the program. When the instruction decoder encounters this symbol, it simply turns off the computer. Note that this is the first instruction which we have required strictly for control purposes.

The functioning of the control unit is illustrated quite well even with this simple program. The particular operations to be performed, and the order in which they are to be done, are specified by the program, and then the control unit directs all the setting of switches and initiation of actions to actually carry out these operations.

We have made several assumptions in writing this program. First, since we used the symbol for BINADD when we instructed that the numbers be added, we assumed that the numbers which were read were represented in binary notation. If the input cards used any other notation, our answer would be wrong. Secondly, we assumed that the accumulator contained zero to start with since the first number was added to the number in the accumulator. If the previous user of the computer left another number in the accumulator, our answer would be wrong. It is customary to provide an instruction for clearing the accumulator in order to avoid this kind of trouble. We shall call this instruction CLEAR and use the symbol 011110000000000 to represent it. This is the second one of the additional instructions shown in Table 8-1 which is required strictly for control purposes. In order to avoid getting the wrong answer in case the accumulator did not contain zero to start with, the first instruction in the program should be 011110000000000.

At this stage of its development, our computer can, conceptually, be used to carry out complicated processing very rapidly. However, the programs required would be very cumbersome since if we wanted to add 100 numbers, for example, it would be necessary to expand the above program by including 98 more READ instructions and 98 more BINADD instructions. This work is reduced by providing other ways of "sequencing" through instructions; the modifications described in the next chapter make the control unit a very powerful assistant to the programmer.

CHAPTER 9

STORED-PROGRAM COMPUTERS

The first step in simplifying the job of programming computers was made by John von Neumann, a famous mathematician. He recognized that since the instructions were represented by symbols, they could be processed in the same way that all other symbols could be. For one thing, instead of having to read the program into the control unit one instruction at a time through a special input device, the instructions could be read in through the standard input device all at once and stored in the computer memory. Each instruction is stored in one word of the memory with consecutive instructions being stored in consecutive locations in the memory. This eliminates the need for a special card reader and thus makes the computer cheaper, but we shall see shortly that it also has other, more important, advantages.

Since all the instructions are in the memory, it is necessary to have some way of specifying the order in which they are to be performed. To do this, a special circuit, called an *instruction counter,* is put in the control unit to keep track of the location of the instruction which is to be performed next. After each instruction is performed, the number in this counter is increased by 1. The control unit always goes to the memory location indicated by the instruction counter to get its next instruction. Thus, if the instruction counter is initially set to 1, the control unit goes to location 1 for its first instruction. After completing the first instruction, the instruction counter now contains 2; so the control unit goes to location 2 for its second instruction, etc. Consequently, the instructions can still be carried out in a predetermined order even though they are all stored in the memory. Figure 9-1 shows

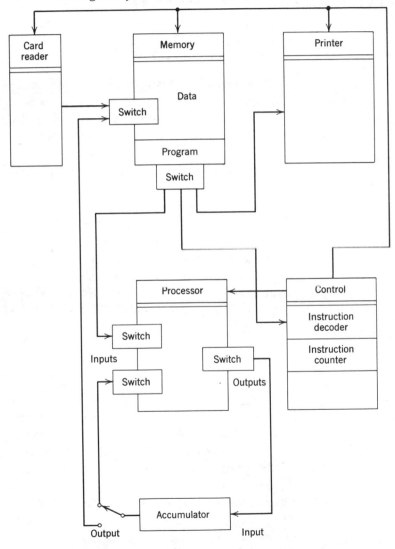

Figure 9-1   Block diagram of stored-program computer.

a block diagram of our revised computer, which is now referred to as a *stored-program* computer because the program is stored in the computer memory.

Although this appears to be a rather minor modification of the computer's organization, it actually has a revolutionary effect because the instructions can be processed just like other symbols. In particular, we can do what is called *address modification*. For example, suppose we want to use the THC 1 to read in 100 numbers so that they can be added, and further suppose that we have decided to place these numbers in locations 400 to 499. The first instruction will be 010010110010000, which says READ 400; that is, read a number into location 400. Now the next instruction that we want is 010010110010001 since this instruction will read the next number into location 401. Note that if we interpret these symbols as binary numbers rather than instructions, the second is just 1 more than the first! This suggests that instead of writing the second instruction, we can construct it by adding 1 to the first instruction. To do this, we could store the first instruction in memory location 1 and store a binary representation for the number 1 in another location, say location 12. Now if we add the numbers in location 1 and 12, we shall get the symbol corresponding to the desired instruction. We could then store this result in some other location, and we would have the second instruction for our desired program. A slight digression is necessary at this point since to make use of this technique, we find that we need a new kind of control instruction and the corresponding operation, called a *branch* or *transfer instruction*. Remember, we agreed that to get its next instruction, the control unit would normally go to the memory location immediately following the location where it got its last instruction. However, we can introduce a new instruction GOTO N which tells the control unit to go to memory location N for its next instruction. Notice that this is another operation which does nothing to symbols representing data; it doesn't add, or read, or write; it simply directs the control unit. When the instruction decoder encounters one of these instructions, it simply sets the instruction counter to the value of N and then asks for its next instruction. Lo and behold, the instruction counter says go to location N for your next instruction! In Table 1 of the last chapter, we anticipated this instruction and used 01101 to represent the operation portion of the instruction GOTO N.

Let us now return to our problem of reading in 100 numbers. After we have constructed the second READ instruction, we can store it in the same location in which the first instruction was found and use a transfer instruction to instruct the computer to go there for its next instruction. Our program is now the following:

Table 9-1 Program illustrating a "loop"

Memory location	Instruction	Explanation
1	010010110010000	Read a number into location 400
2	011110000000000	Clear the accumulator
3	110010000000001	Add the symbol in location 1 to the accumulator
4	110010000001100	Add the number in location 12 to the accumulator
5	010110000000001	Store the symbol in the accumulator in location 1
6	011010000000001	GOTO location 1 for next instruction
12	000000000000001	Binary number 1

Now let's see what happens when the computer starts to "run" this program. During the first instruction time, it reads the first number into location 400. During the second, third, fourth, and fifth instruction times, it calculates the instruction which tells it to read a number into location 401 and stores that instruction into location 1. During the sixth instruction time, it finds that it should go to location 1 for its next instruction but does nothing else. During the seventh instruction time, the second input number is read into location 401. During the eighth, ninth, tenth, and eleventh times, it calculates the instruction which tells it to read a number into location 402, and then it stores that instruction back into location 1, etc. We see that this short six-word program is a *loop* which will run on and on, reading new numbers into consecutive memory locations at the rate of one number per six instruction times.

This simple program illustrates the tremendous power of the branch instruction to relieve the programmer from the task of specifying each individual operation of the computer. Since a modern high-speed computer can carry out on the order of a million operations in a second, it would take a very long time to write the program for even 1 second of computing if each operation in the program had to be specified separately. However, by just writing these six instructions (plus the constant one in location 12), the programmer can cause the computer to store many thousand numbers in the memory in a fraction of a second. Actually, since card readers tend to be slow, this program would be limited in speed by the card reader. However, the ability of the programmer to use loops in this way is an extremely important consequence of branch instructions.

To help visualize the operation of programs such as these, it is customary to draw a *flow diagram* which indicates the order in which the computer will carry out the instructions of the program. A flow diagram corresponding to this program is shown in Figure 9-2. We shall discuss such diagrams in more detail in the next chapter.

If we examine the flow diagram carefully, we see that there is a fatal defect in this program which must be corrected before we try to run it; there is no way out of the loop! After going around the loop 100 times and thus reading in the 100 numbers we wanted, the computer just keeps on going looking for a one hundred and first number. Clearly, we need some kind of instruction which will enable us to terminate the loop after just 100 numbers have been read. To do this, we need an instruction called a *conditional transfer* or *conditional branch*.

Our first branch instruction, the GOTO, is called an *unconditional branch* since the control unit goes to the specified location for its next

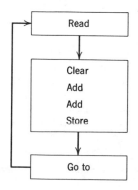

Figure 9-2   Flow diagram of program loop.

instruction under all conditions. The new instruction, which we shall call GZGOTO *N*, tells the control unit to go to memory location *N* for its next instruction *provided* that the accumulator contains a number Greater than Zero. More briefly, we say that control is transferred to location *N* if the accumulator is greater than zero. If the accumulator does contain zero, or a number less than zero, to find its next instruction, the control unit simply goes on to the location immediately following the one where the GZGOTO was found. Let's see how such a conditional-transfer instruction can be used.

Let us assume that the number one hundred in binary notation is in location 13 at the start of the run. Each time we go through the loop, we shall subtract 1 from the number in location 13 and check to see whether the result is zero. If not, we store the result in location 13 and start around the loop again. After the one hundredth time through the loop, the result of the subtraction is zero, and instead of going back to the beginning of the loop, we continue on for our next instruction. Let's make that a HALT instruction so that the computer will stop and await further instructions. The resulting program is shown in Table 9-2 and the corresponding flow diagram in Figure 9-3.

At last we have a workable program! By using just 13 symbols

Table 9-2 Program for reading 100 input numbers

Memory location	Symbol	Explanation
1	010010110010000	Read a number into location 400
2	011110000000000	Clear the accumulator
3	110010000000001	Add the symbol in location 1 to the accumulator
4	110010000001100	Add the number in location 12 to the accumulator
5	010110000000001	Store the symbol in the accumulator in location 1
6	011110000000000	Clear the accumulator
7	110010000001101	Add the number in location 13 to the accumulator
8	110100000001100	Subtract the number in location 12 from the accumulator
9	010110000001101	Store the result in location 13
10	011100000000001	If the accumulator is not zero, go to location 1 for next instruction
11	111110000000000	Halt
12	000000000000001	Binary representation of 1
13	000000001100100	Binary representation of 100

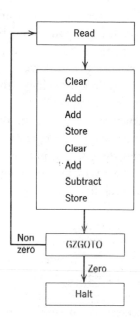

Figure 9-3   Flow diagram for
input program.

(and just 13 memory locations), we have obtained a program which will read in precisely 100 numbers and put them in the locations we specified, i.e., locations 400 to 499. Without the ability to loop and branch, we would have had to write down more than 100 instructions and would have used up a corresponding number of memory locations. The resulting saving of both programming effort and memory space is very significant in increasing the usefulness and power of computers. In the illustration, the number of instructions is reduced by a factor of about 6; i.e., only 13 instructions were written to perform 100 operations. However, it is not at all unusual to have loops with even fewer instructions traversed millions of times whenever a program is run so that even larger reductions in the necessary work are obtained.

This very short program illustrates several interesting ways in which the designer and programmer of computers interact. First, we observe that twice we used the CLEAR operation followed by an ADD. This is not necessary since the computer designer has very thoughtfully provided us with a FETCH operation which achieves the same result in one step. Thus the second and third steps in the program could be replaced with the single operation FETCH 1, i.e., fetch the contents of location 1 to the accumulator. There are frequently many ways in which the programmer can use the available operations to achieve the desired result, and it is his job to choose the most efficient.

In order to help the programmer write efficient programs, the designers examine typical programs to determine what types of operations are needed. After examining the program, the designer would point out to the programmer that he should be using the FETCH instruction, but then he might also observe that a sequence of five instructions is being used to carry out a READ instruction and then increase the address in that instruction by 1. This suggests providing a special circuit (called an *index register*) which, just after an instruction is carried out, adds 1 to the address part of that instruction; this provides a considerable reduction of running time and program length for many programs. Thus, by adding extra circuits and providing special instructions to carry out frequently used and important processes, the designer makes it possible for the programmer to write much shorter and faster programs.

We shall not define any of these special instructions for the THC 1 since the set we have available is adequate for our purposes. However, one additional control instruction, another conditional transfer called the LZGOTO, is listed in Table 8-10. This instruction is just like GZGOTO except that control is transferred to location N if the accumulator *is* zero, or Less than Zero, rather than if it is greater than zero. Actually, only one of these conditional-transfer instructions is necessary, but it is considerably more convenient at times to have them both available.

Having completed our listing of control operations, we can now conclude the discussion of the control unit. The major difference in the operation of the control circuit of a stored-program computer as compared with the operation described in the last chapter is that the instructions are obtained from the computer memory rather than from an input device connected to the control unit. After obtaining the instruction, the control unit decodes it and carries it out just as described earlier. As was mentioned earlier, an instruction counter is added to the control unit in order to keep track of where the next instruction is to be obtained. By manipulating the setting of this instruction counter, the control unit can carry out conditional or unconditional transfers from one place to another in a program. Thus, a stored-program computer can carry out instructions in very complicated sequences rather than just in the order in which the instructions are written down. This makes the computers much more powerful and easier to use.

To really understand the functioning of the control unit, it is helpful to simulate the operation of the computer while running some program, e.g., the program of Table 9-2. Table 9-3 illustrates how this may be done with the aid of a table, which is used to keep track of changes in the computer. (The table does not show memory locations 2 to 12 since their contents do not change while the program is run.) This table assumes that the computer is ready to run a program which is identical to that of Table 9-2 except that only three numbers are to be read in. Consequently, the symbols in memory locations 1 to 13 are just those shown in Table 9-2 except that the symbol in location 13 is a binary 3 rather than a binary one hundred since only three numbers are to be read in. Before the program begins (time 0), the instruction counter is set to 1 since the first instruction of the program is in memory location 1. We do not know the contents of the accumulator or memory locations 400, 401, and 402 since we do not know what the computer was used for previously. After the first instruction is carried out (time 1), the instruction counter is set to 2, and a number (let's assume it was 0) has been transmitted from the card reader to location 400. The dashes indicate that the contents of the other registers are unchanged. After the second instruction, the accumulator has been cleared, the instruction counter set to 3, and nothing else changed. Similarly, the changes due to the first 15 operations are shown in the figure. After the thirtieth operation, the computer will halt with the memory contents shown (assuming that the numbers to be read in were 0, 1, and 2). It should be very beneficial to complete the table and see just how the loop is terminated.

This description of the operation of the control unit completes the discussion of the basic organization and operation of a computer. The THC 1, as now defined, constitutes a very simplified, but quite representative, model of a modern digital computer. An understanding of its

Memory Locations

End of Time	Instruction Counter	Accumulator	1	13	400	401	402
0	1	?	0100101100010000	0000000000000011	?	?	?
1	2	—	—	—	—	—	—
2	3	0000000000000000	—	—	0000000000000000	—	—
3	4	0100101100100000	—	—	—	—	—
4	5	0100101100100001	—	—	—	—	—
5	6	—	0100101100010001	—	—	—	—
6	7	0000000000000000	—	—	—	—	—
7	8	0000000000000011	—	—	—	—	—
8	9	0000000000000010	—	0000000000000010	—	—	—
9	10	—	—	—	—	—	—
10	1	—	—	—	—	—	—
11	2	0000000000000000	—	—	—	0000000000000001	—
12	3	0101010110010001	—	—	—	—	—
13	4	0101010110010010	—	—	—	—	—
14	5	—	0100101100010010	—	—	—	—
15	6						
16	7						
17	8						
18	9						
19	10						
20	1						
21	2						
22	3						
23	4						
24	5						
25	6						
26	7						
27	8						
28	9						
29	10	0000000000000000	0101011001010011	0000000000000000	0000000000000000	0000000000000001	0000000000000010
30	11	0000000000000000	0101011001010011	0000000000000000	0000000000000000	0000000000000001	0000000000000010

Table 9-3 Sequence of computer operations during execution of a program.

basic operations and the methods by which the sequence of operations is controlled provides an accurate picture of much more complicated machines.

Since it is now clear that a program is very important to the use of a computer, we shall devote the next chapter to discussing how a program is produced. We shall see that, although programming can be a very difficult task, it is possible to use the computer to simplify the job substantially.

CHAPTER 10

PROGRAMMING

A *program* has been defined earlier as a sequence of instructions to be carried out by the computer. The *programmer* is the person who analyzes a particular job to be done on a computer and specifies a sequence of instructions to do the job. How does he proceed in this task?

The first step requires specifying in great detail exactly what is the job to be done. This is frequently the most difficult part of the job since it is not unusual to find when we start to consider a problem closely that we do not know what the problem is. For example, suppose a programmer is asked to write a program to determine the optimum price for a new product. What is optimum? Well, let's say the price that produces the maximum profit. What determines the profit? Well, the cost per unit, the price per unit, and the number of units sold. What determines the number of units sold? Well, the psychological reaction of people to the product, the package, the price, and general economic conditions. What determines these things? We don't know. So the programmer is stopped before he really gets started.

If the problem analysis can be carried out, the programmer determines exactly what the input data will consist of, what the relations between the input and output are under all possible conditions, and exactly what the output information is to be.

The programmer must then select an *algorithm,* i.e., a sequence of specific steps, by which the desired output information can be obtained from the input data. This choice is an important part of his job since it plays a major role in determining how difficult the program will be to write and how long the computer will have to run in order to solve the problem. Since both programmers and computers cost money, it is very desirable that both the programming time and the running time be as short as possible.

The algorithm chosen by the programmer consists of a sequence of steps, each of which is ordinarily much simpler than the initial problem. Of course, if the initial problem is very complex, each step may be so complicated that it must be broken down into a simpler sequence of steps. In any case, each step in the sequence will require that a program be written to carry it out; the problem is ultimately broken down into small enough steps so that each of these programs is easily written.

If the problem is at all complicated, the number of individual steps can be very large, and their relationship is hard to keep clear. Furthermore, it is not very easy to analyze a sequence of instructions and recognize very clearly just what individual steps are involved. It is very important that the algorithm be specified precisely and unambiguously, and the English language, or any other for that matter, is not completely satisfactory for this purpose. As a simple example, consider the direction to "subtract five from twenty four times." Is the result 0, or is it 15 all four times? Many other similar ambiguities can be constructed easily, and we are all familiar with instances of misunderstood instructions. For these reasons a program is commonly described by means of a *flow diagram* or *flow chart.* This diagram identifies the individual steps involved in the program and depicts graphically their relationship. Let us consider a simple example to illustrate the use of such diagrams.

We have been asked to write a program to compute, for each person on a payroll, the weekly wage. The input data consists of the name, number of hours worked, the normal rate of pay, and the rate of pay for any hours worked over 40, for each person on the payroll. We are asked to print a list showing each person's name and his total wages.

After satisfying ourselves that we know exactly what the job is, our next step is to select an algorithm for doing it. The following flow chart shows one possible algorithm.

The particular sequence of steps we have chosen starts by reading in the data for one person. The next box (a diamond-shaped figure) indicates that we are to determine whether or not this person worked more than 40 hours. Note that we can exit from this box on either of two branches; this implies that the program for carrying out this step will use at least one conditional-branch instruction. It is customary to use a diamond-shaped figure for this kind of step in order to emphasize that there is a decision involved, i.e., that conditional branching is involved. If the man has worked more than 40 hours, we go on to the box on the top right and compute his overtime pay. We then add to this amount his pay for the first 40 hours of work and print out the results. If the man did not work more than 40 hours, we calculate his wage and then print the result. Following this, we check to see whether we have completed the payroll. If not, we return to the beginning and start around the loop once more.

This is the first example we have seen in which the computer is making a clear-cut, albeit trivial, decision; a slight digression from our

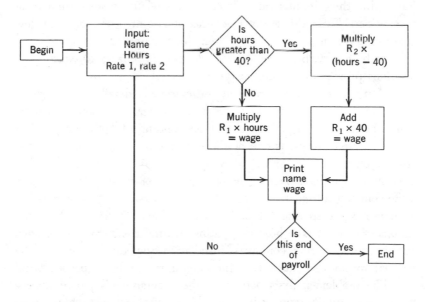

Figure 10-1   Flow chart for computation of weekly wage.

discussion of programming is in order to clarify and amplify this important aspect of computer applications. Notice that the programmer cannot make the decision as to which of the two means of calculating the wage should be used since the choice depends on whether or not more than 40 hours were worked. This piece of information is not available until the program is run and varies from person to person; consequently, the computer must decide which is the proper procedure. Of course, it is very easily done in this case; but even though more complicated criteria may be necessary, programs can be written to allow the computer to make decisions based on the available data.

One last point before we return to the discussion of programming—to avoid anyone drawing a misleading conclusion from the fact that in our flow chart the only "decisions" made involved questions which could be answered yes or no—let us hasten to point out that branching is possible into any number of distinct program branches. It is not at all unusual to have a decision made by a computer on the basis of a question which has many possible answers. Don't be misled into thinking that because a computer uses binary devices, it can only make binary decisions! Someone might say "Yes, the decisions aren't strictly binary, but the computer can only consider a relatively small number of possibilities." Even this is not true since it is quite common in a flow chart to have many consecutive branching points. Decisions do not have to be binary, but even if every decision is binary, 20 consecutive decisions provide over a million possible cases!

Many people are surprised at the extremely detailed specification of the steps required to produce a computer program for solving a problem. The need for a very precise understanding of both the problem and a solution process is one of the outstanding characteristics of the application and programming of computers. It is very common to find that understanding is lacking in one or both of these areas; it is also quite common to find that once sufficient understanding is obtained, a computer is not necessary! This has been particularly true in the applications of computers to business routine. A careful system study carried out preliminary to a computer installation sometimes improves the manual routines so much that the computer can be dispensed with!

The problem-analysis portion of the programmer's job requires a very broad and thorough education. If the problem is highly mathematical, rather sophisticated mathematics may be needed to determine how to make the calculation so as to get a sufficiently accurate result. If the problem involves business-data processing, the programmer may have to learn a great deal about how the business is organized in order to produce a practical program. Generally a college education is required for jobs of this sort.

Let us go on to consider in a little more detail how the programs corresponding to individual steps of the algorithm are produced. In the preceding chapter we saw some examples of actual programs. These were written in *machine language;* i.e., the program instructions were written using the symbols which actually represent the instructions in the machine. In the early days of stored-program computers, programming was actually done this way, but now this is almost never done because it is slow and highly susceptible to programming errors. Simply trying to copy one of the short programs given in the previous chapter should be convincing evidence of this!

The first step in simplifying the programming job was the substitution of mnemonics for the binary symbols representing the operations and the use of decimal integers for the address portion of the instructions. Thus, instead of writing 110010000000010, the programmer writes BINADD 2. He finds it easier to remember that BINADD corresponds to the operation of adding two numbers in binary notation, and he is not so likely to make a mistake in writing the location of the number to be added either. Naturally, before the computer can use a program written with these mnemonic instructions, they must be translated into machine-language instructions. This translation is rather straightforward since it essentially involves just a substitution of the symbols on the right-hand side of Table 8-1 for those on the left-hand side. We shall see how this is done very shortly.

The next step in simplifying the programming was considerably more difficult to carry out, but not hard to understand. Usually a programmer does not care exactly where a symbol is to be put; he only wishes to ensure that it be stored somewhere. In such cases, programmers are allowed to use a *symbolic address* rather than specify precisely the memory location in which a piece of data is to be stored. For example, consider the first instruction of our program for reading 100 numbers (see Table 9-2). As written it was 010010110010000; if we had used mnemonic instructions, we could have written it more simply as READ 400. Using symbolic addresses, it can be written even more simply as READ DATALOC where DATALOC is a mnemonic for the *location* where the first piece of *data* is to be stored. To refer to this location in any other instruction, and we undoubtedly shall if we are going to do anything useful with the data, the name DATALOC can be used; we are thus less likely to put the data some place and then later on to confuse that location with some other. A program written with instructions of this sort, i.e., symbolic addresses and mnemonics for the operations, is called a *symbolic program* or *assembly-language program*. As an example, Table 10-1 shows the symbolic program corresponding to the machine-language program in Table 9-2.

As we mentioned earlier, there must be some way to translate a symbolic program to an actual sequence of machine-language instructions since this is the only representation of machine operations for which the designers planned. What is more natural than to use the computer to do this translation! The basic process involved is strictly symbol manipulation, i.e., the translation of the mnemonics used in the symbolic program into the strings of 0s and 1s used to represent machine-language instructions. Of course, it is necessary to write a program which directs the computer while it is carrying out this translation process. A particular program, called an *assembler,* or sometimes a *translator,* is written for each computer. The assembler program accepts

Table 10-1 Symbolic program for reading 100 numbers

INSTRU	READ	DATALOC
	CLEAR	
	BINADD	INSTRU
	BINADD	ONE
	STORE	INSTRU
	CLEAR	
	BINADD	INDEX
	BINSUB	ONE
	STORE	INDEX
	GZGOTO	INSTRU
	HALT	
ONE	000000000000001	
INDEX	000000001100100	

any symbolic program as input data; it produces as output a program written in machine language. This output program is usually obtained in the form of a deck of punched cards since it will subsequently be used as input to the computer. The programmer keeps this output program until he is ready to use it; then he takes the machine-language program and the input data and runs it on the computer to get his desired output. Thus, the computer is used at least twice for each program, once to translate the symbolic program into machine language and once to run the program and get the results. This process is illustrated in Figure 10-2.

Since an assembler program produces just one machine-language instruction for each mnemonic instruction, the programmer must still write down each instruction. This limitation was overcome by the next step in simplifying programming which was the development of *compilers* and *problem-oriented languages*. Programmers observed that for a given class of problems certain steps occurred very frequently. For example, in our problem to compute weekly wages, we used a step in which we computed the wage W by multiplying the hours H times the rate R; this can be expressed by the formula $W = H \times R$. Many problems involve simple arithmetical computations of this sort and also procedures such as "Do the following statements 100 times." Consequently, a compiler program was written which can translate these statements into sequences of symbolic instructions. For example, if the statement

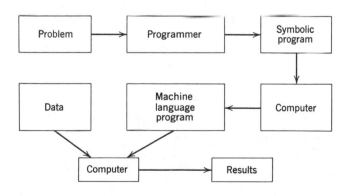

Figure 10-2   Schematic indication of symbolic programming.

$W = H \times R$ is provided as input data to this compiler program, it produces as output the sequence of symbolic instructions:

CLEAR
BINADD H
BINMUL R
STORE W

This sequence of instructions can then be translated by the assembler program to a sequence of machine-language instructions.

The input program supplied to the compiler or translator is usually referred to as the *source program*. The overall process of producing and running a machine-language program from a source program is summarized schematically in Figure 10-3.   (Note: The compiler sometimes translates the source program directly into machine-language instructions; i.e., the assembler is included within the compiler.)

By using an appropriate problem-oriented language, the number of statements which the programmer must write may be less than a tenth of the number of machine instructions which are required. The best known compiler for a language of this sort is called FORTRAN for *formula translator*. It is very well suited to arithmetical calculations.

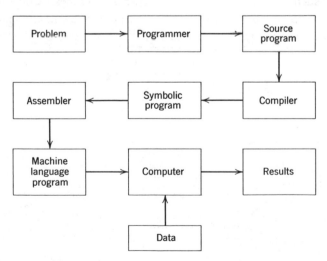

Figure 10-3   Schematic indication of use of problem-oriented language.

Table 10-2

1		READ	NUMBER
2	BEGIN	READ	NAME
3		READ	HOURS
4		READ	RATE 1
5		READ	RATE 2
6		FETCH	HOURS
7		WRSUB	FORTY
8		GZGOTO	EXTRA
9		FETCH	RATE 1
10		WRMUL	HOURS
11		STORE	WAGES
12		GOTO	OUT
13	EXTRA	WRMUL	RATE 2
14		STORE	WAGES
15		FETCH	RATE 1
16		WRMUL	FORTY
17		WRADD	WAGES
18		STORE	WAGES
19	OUT	PRINT	NAME
20		PRINT	WAGES
21	TEST	FETCH	NUMBER
22		BINSUB	ONE
23		STORE	NUMBER
24		GZGOTO	BEGIN
25		HALT	
26	ONE		
27	FORTY		

As an illustration of the difference between an assembly language or symbolic program and a program written in a FORTRAN-like language, Tables 10-2 and 10-3 illustrate programs corresponding to the flow chart for the payroll problem. We shall not discuss these programs in detail, but the reduction in the number of statements from 27 to 9 is obviously desirable from the programmer's viewpoint. (Since we have not specified an assembler or a compiler for the THC 1, it is not possible to describe in detail the conversion of either of these programs into a machine-language program; for this simple program it would actually be quite easy with the exception of the input-output part of the program. Because of the extremely limited facilities assumed for the THC 1, this part would be somewhat complicated. As a matter of fact,

Table 10-3

1		READ NUMBER
2		DO I = 1, NUMBER
3		READ NAME(I), HOURS(I), RATE 1(I), RATE 2(I)
4		OVERTIME = HOURS − 40.0
5		IF (OVERTIME) REGULAR, REGULAR, EXTRA
6	REGULAR	WAGES = HOURS * RATE 1
7		GOTO OUT
8	EXTRA	WAGES = OVERTIME * RATE 2 + 40.0 * RATE 1
9	OUT	PRINT NAME, WAGES

it frequently happens for real computers that input and output are the most complicated portion of the program.)

A concept which is very useful to programmers in reducing their work is that of a *subroutine*. A subroutine is a program which can, with few alterations, be used many times within other programs. For example, a THC 1 programmer might find that he frequently wants to read a list of numbers and store them in the computer memory. Examination of the program given in Table 9-2 discloses that it can be changed very easily to read any number of numbers and store them any place in the memory. All that is necessary is that the memory location where the first number is to be stored should be put in the address part of the first instruction, and the number of numbers in the list should be put in memory location 13. Hence, the programmer needs only to write this program once, and then anytime he wants to use it, he simply inserts the correct numbers in these two instructions. In addition to simplifying the programming job, subroutines save memory space since the entire program does not have to be stored every time it is needed.

Another very important aid to the programmer is the existence of a program *library*. This library is a collection of subroutines and other programs which have been written by many programmers and are made available for anyone to use. Thus, if the programmer chooses his algorithm properly, many of the steps may already be programmed. He can obtain programs from the library for these steps and then write the additional parts for which library programs are not available.

Most computer manufacturers now provide a large number of programs to a customer when they deliver the computer itself—the hardware. These programs are commonly referred to as *software* by analogy with the term *hardware*. Among these programs are likely to be assemblers, special-purpose compilers, large libraries of subroutines, a monitor system (discussed in Chapter 12), and others. Since a computer is absolutely no use without programs and since this software is vitally important in determining how easily and rapidly other programs can be written, the quality of the software is just as important as the quality of the hardware in determining the usefulness of the computer. It is not at all uncommon for a user to select a computer on the basis of the software that is available rather than the hardware. Consequently, computer manufacturers put as much thought, and frequently more manpower, into the design of the software as into the design of the hardware.

No discussion of programming would be complete without mentioning *debugging*. Since it is very difficult for a human to write an entire program without making any mistakes, almost invariably the first time a program is run, it does not perform properly. The programmer then has the challenging job of locating and correcting the mistakes. Of course, the computer is called in to give him assistance! Diagnostic programs can print out messages to the programmer which provide him with clues as to where the errors may be. For example, suppose in the program given in Table 10-2, the statement READ RATE 1 had been omitted by the programmer. Later on in the program RATE 1 is referred to several times, but at no place is its value either calculated or obtained as input. The assembler would recognize that something is wrong although, of course, it could not determine exactly what the programmer had intended. Consequently the assembler would print out a comment such as "RATE 1 IS AN UNDEFINED SYMBOL," and then the programmer would have to figure out what was wrong. In this case, he would probably see immediately that he had intended to obtain this as input and would just add the missing READ statement to the program. Even with this type of assistance, it may require longer to "debug" a program than to write it.

This concludes our description of the principal techniques which have been developed to aid the programmer in his task. It should be clear at this point that a computer is useless without the proper programs, and, indeed, it is true that "a computer does only what a programmer tells it to do"—an often-heard remark about computers. However, this remark is also somewhat misleading. Consider, for example, the flow chart of Figure 10-1. This is, of course, a very simple job. More complicated programs may require flow charts which involve thousands of boxes with each box representing a program more complicated than this entire program. If you can imagine a flow diagram illustrating such a program, you can see why the statement that a computer "does only what a programmer tells it to do" may be misleading. These programs may be written by many people, and usually they are written and tested as separate subroutines so that the debugging problem is eased. For a big problem, this programming job may take months or years. Consequently, it is, in fact, impossible for any one person to predict exactly what the computer will do in any given circumstance.

In a somewhat less trivial sense, consider a large complicated program written by a single programmer. Although the programmer does specify all possible branches and each individual step, he finds it impossible to consider in detail all possible behaviors for arbitrary input data. Consequently, the programmer is likely to be as surprised as anyone else after the program is run; we shall mention some interesting examples later. Of course, once the result has been produced, the programmer is usually able to examine the input data and determine just how this result occurred. However, in some instances, even this is not possible in any practical sense since it might require years of work, without a single mistake by the programmer, to figure out exactly what happened.

Some numbers may help to make this point even clearer. It was stated earlier that an operation in a large, high-speed computer can be carried out in about a millionth of a second. If a program runs for an hour on this computer (which is longer than average, but many programs run even longer), it would take the programmer more than a century to trace this sequence of steps *doing one operation each second*. Of course, the programmer may well find some shortcuts, but on the other hand he simply can't continue this kind of detailed analysis very long without making a mistake. Consequently, the programmer is usually willing to be surprised and let the machine produce the evidence as to what is being done.

By way of summary, the following points are worth remembering.

1. A general-purpose computer is worthless without programs. The job of programming a computer to carry out a task properly and efficiently is an important one. The programmer must have a very deep understanding of the problem in order to write a good program, and the process of choosing the algorithm to be used in the program is one of the most important parts of programming.

2. The machine-language program which controls the computer while it is carrying out a specific task is extremely detailed and depends on each step being precisely defined.

3. Techniques have been developed to use computers to aid in programming computers. Assemblers, compilers, and problem-oriented languages allow the programmer to write his program using fewer and simpler statements which are then translated into the final machine language program.

4. The availability of subroutines and program libraries simplifies the programming task by allowing many people to use the same program and by allowing one program to be used many times.

5. Although a computer does do "only what a programmer tells it to do," the programmer may not know what he told it to do in any very precise sense.

CHAPTER 11

APPLICATIONS OF COMPUTERS

In this chapter we shall discuss some of the characteristics of computers which make them appropriate for certain applications and the characteristics of a job which make it amenable to computer solutions, and we shall illustrate both of these with some examples. Perhaps the first thing we should do is to reconsider the examples given back in Chapter 2 and see whether, in light of our greater knowledge of computers, those jobs really were suitable for computers. The first problem we considered was the alphabetizing of all the words on the front page of a newspaper. It is clear that we can use a card punch to put each of the words on a card and then use a simple program to read all of the words into the computer memory. A little thought would lead us to an algorithm for sorting, or rearranging the words in memory, so that they are in alphabetical order. (Although it is very easy to find an algorithm which will work, sorting is such an important process and can be so time consuming that programmers have put a lot of effort into developing very fast, efficient programs which are available in most program libraries. Consequently, we probably would not even have to write this part of the program ourselves because a suitable program would probably be available.) Then, after the words have been ordered, another very simple program would suffice to have them printed in that order. In a modern computer center such a program would be trivial to write and would require less than a minute to run on a large computer. The biggest part of the job would be the typing of the entire page, but it would still be a great deal simpler and faster than doing the sorting manually.

The second example we considered in Chapter 2 was a simple multiplication problem, and we could easily write a program to do this on the THC 1 computer. In fact, a suitable program is shown in Table 11-1.

However, if we consider the time necessary to write the program and to punch the numbers on cards, it is quite unlikely that we could get the answer anywhere near as fast as we could do the multiplication on a blackboard! Hence, we conclude that the first problem is well suited to computers (even though it involves little or no numerical computation) and that the second is not.

Evidently there are many factors which determine whether a job is well suited to a computer, and to help simplify their consideration, we shall classify computer applications according to the primary reason for using a computer to do the job. Basically, a computer can be used for one, or more, of the following reasons: to gain economy, to make the job feasible at all, or to achieve insight into some process. We shall discuss each of these more fully by considering some examples.

As our first example, let us consider the preparation of the weekly payroll of a large company. The basic job is the preparation of a check for the appropriate amount of money. This amount of money is determined by the number of hours worked, the normal and overtime rate for this person, his payments for social security and income tax, and any other amounts to be withheld, e.g., hospitalization payments.

In order to prepare the check, weekly data is needed specifying

Table 11-1 Symbolic program
for multiplying two numbers

READ	N1
READ	N2
FETCH	N1
BINMUL	N2
STORE	N3
PRINT	N3

the hours worked by each person on the payroll. In addition, the computer must have the following more-or-less fixed data available for each person: (1) name; (2) department or address; (3) hourly rate for normal time; (4) hourly rate for overtime; (5) number of income-tax exemptions; (6) social security paid so far this year; (7) amount of weekly hospitalization payment, if any. All this fixed information can be recorded on a master file which is usually a magnetic tape. It can be used over and over and thus does not have to be supplied every week on punched cards or some other relatively more expensive form of input. Once a week, therefore, the master file together with the weekly-hours-worked data (probably recorded on punched cards) serves as input data for the program which computes the amount of the check. This computation is considerably more complicated than the simple wage computation illustrated in the previous chapter, but it is still a relatively simple one. It would probably take a clerk about a minute to do and a medium-size computer about a thousandth of a second.

This program has at least two kinds of output. First, it may make some changes in the master tape; for example, if additional social security was withheld, it increases the amount withheld during this year. Second, it actually produces the checks. Generally this would be done by having some intermediate output (perhaps tape) generated which is used in turn to control a check-writing machine.

Although the information on the master file is relatively fixed, it does change occasionally; the man might be transferred to a different department, get a salary increase, or increase the number of his income-tax exemptions. Consequently, in addition to the actual wage computation another program is needed to edit the master file and bring all this information up to date. This change information is placed on punched cards and accumulated during each week. Shortly before the program to produce the weekly checks is run, this data is supplied to the edit program, and the master file is updated. It is then ready for use in the check computation. The overall process is illustrated in Figure 11-1.

The major objective of using the computer in such applications as these is simply economy. There are sometimes other objectives; e.g., fewer people are required; payroll production is faster and more accurate; but almost always the primary objective is to reduce the costs. Of

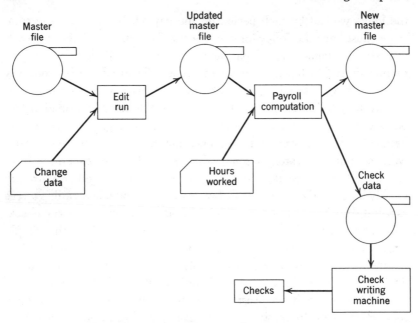

Figure 11-1   Flow chart of weekly payroll preparation.

course, the costs of preparing and maintaining the master tape file and writing all the programs must be considered. However, since the program is used every week and relatively few changes have to be made to the master file, these costs are small enough so that large savings are possible. Actual figures for a representative company indicated that the costs were reduced by a factor of three.

One of the important characteristics of most applications of computers is discernible even in this brief description of an extremely oversimplified version of the job to be done. Although the task itself is simple—the program for computing the amount of the check requires only 10 or 20 instructions—there are many associated details which must be taken care of, e.g., reprogramming for tax-rate changes, obtaining information about changes of address, storing the tapes used for the master files, etc. Careful planning and execution of the entire process is essential if the system is to be successful since these associated "details" may well be controlling in determining how economically and efficiently the system functions.

This application illustrates some other important characteristics of one class of problems suited to computers. First, the amount of input data which must be manually prepared for each run is reasonable. If all the information on the master file had to be supplied manually each week, it is unlikely that there would be any savings. In other words, if the objective is economy, and it is more work to prepare the input data than it is to do the computation, don't do it on a computer! Second, much of the data, and the program itself, can be used over and over. Although this is a relatively simple program, the cost of writing it is much larger than the cost of preparing one of the weekly payrolls. It is only because the programming costs can be spread over many uses of the program that it is economical. Third, the problem itself involves many repetitions of a fairly simple job. This is almost a *sine qua non* of jobs suited to computers; if the job, or some substantial part of it, is not highly repetitious, then it probably is not economically done on a computer.

There are many industrial and business jobs with similar characteristics which are now being done on computers at greatly reduced costs. Preparing sales reports, controlling inventory, billing, preparing parts lists, and many others are all applications for which a major objective is economy. However, there are other applications which are characterized not by the resulting savings, but by the fact that the jobs would not be *feasible* if they had to be done without using computers. Let us consider this class of applications next.

An excellent illustration of this type of application of computers is in the forecasting of weather. Because of its direct and obvious importance to man, predicting the weather (or formulating rules which attempt to minimize its adverse effects on such activities as crop planting) was probably one of the first technological questions to be attacked. Before the turn of the century, a mathematical model of the atmosphere including the equations which describe how the relevant variables such as air pressure, temperature, humidity, and velocity change over a period of time was formulated. At least as long ago as 1911, it was pointed out that the weather could be predicted by solving these equations. If the pressure, temperature, humidity, and velocity of the air are known for the same instant of time at many points around the world, the solution of the equations is mathematically quite straightforward and accurately predicts what these quantities will be 1 hour, 1 day, or 1 week later. A network of weather stations around the world can make the measurements necessary to provide the initial conditions for these calculations, but it happens that a tremendous number of numerical calculations are required. Without a computer these computations required months of work, and there was obviously no point to predicting the weather, if the weather was already over! Consequently, this proposal lay essentially dormant until the advent of high-speed computers.

Immediately after it became clear that digital computers would vastly speed up such calculations, mathematicians and meterologists intensified study of this method of prediction. Although the first results were crude, by 1962 a useful system was in routine operation. This system uses about 2,000 measurement reports to establish the initial conditions and then a large, high-speed computer requires 1 hour to make a 1-day prediction. More computation is required to make predictions over a longer period of time.

Although there is ample evidence that weather predictions are still not 100 percent accurate, these numerical predictions have increased the accuracy of certain forecasts quite significantly. However, the primary point of interest to us at this time is that this method of prediction was not even feasible before the advent of computers because the tremendous number of calculations required the very high speed of modern computers in order to obtain the results rapidly enough for them to be at all interesting.

A second important characteristic of this problem is that a very long sequence of calculations must be carried out with no mistakes. It would not do to make 100 million individual correct calculations (which is the order of magnitude involved in a 1-day forecast) and then to make a mistake on the last one and so predict rain on a sunny day, or vice versa. A computer is able to go through a very long error-free sequence whereas it is not possible for a person to take more than a few hundred or few thousand steps before making a mistake. In some applications it is only this high reliability of a computer which makes the job feasible at all.

A third, and distinct, characteristic may not be quite so obvious. In order to reduce the work involved in such calculations, a person would probably "round" the numbers to just a few significant figures and thus simplify the calculation. The computer is able to carry comfortably a very large number of figures so as to obtain very high precision. Another application may make this requirement more clear. When a missile is aimed at the moon, it is necessary to make extensive calculations to determine very small corrections to its course in order to fly close enough to take pictures. Each of these calculations must be carried out using a large number of significant figures in order to come close to a target almost 250,000 miles away.

To make the point again, computers are not used primarily as a means of reducing the cost of analytical weather forecasting. They are used because it is only with the high speed, reliability, and precision of the digital computer that this method is feasible at all.

To digress slightly, this is a good point at which to comment upon the frequently heard remark that "computers can do nothing that we cannot do ourselves." This statement is true only in a very trivial sense. Although, of course, it is possible to carry out exactly the same computations manually as are carried out by the computer, we don't do it because it is not worthwhile. R. W. Hamming has compared this statement with one that, regarded solely as a form of transportation, flying is no different than walking. Yet we all recognize that the drastic reduction in time required to get from one coast to the other via jet plane results in our making the trip many times, but we would never even consider walking the 3,000 miles. Similarly, the even greater increase in the speed and reliability of symbol processing by computer rather than by manual technique results in our doing things by computers that we would not do without them.

Many other jobs are feasible only with the aid of a computer because the output results must be available a very short time after the input data are available. These are called *real-time* applications since the computations must be made, and the results available, on the same time scale as that of the process involved. This contrasts with a job such as the payroll preparation in which the total computation time may well be a very small fraction of the week's time available for getting the results. The control of missile shots is a good example of a real-time computation. In order to put a satellite into a precise orbit, necessary instructions to the rockets, based on data obtained after liftoff, must be supplied at critical points during the launch. Only a computer can make the necessary calculations rapidly enough.

A somewhat more prosaic, but perhaps more important, example of a real-time application is the control of production lines. By continuously monitoring the items being produced, variations from the desired standard can be analyzed in a computer, and changes can be made in some of the production processes to reduce these variations. These are called *process-control* applications, and computers are now being used in this manner in oil refining, cement manufacturing, electronic parts manufacturing, and many other processes. Banking systems are also required to produce some information a very short time after the information is requested. For example, inquiries as to the balance in an account must be answered within minutes, and often a prodigious number of calculations are involved in keeping the balances correct.

Naturally, many computer applications are characterized both by being feasible only with a computer and also by leading to economies. For example, by using a computer to keep records of every item in the inventory of a factory, it may be feasible to reduce the size of the inventory to cover only one week's work without any appreciable danger of running out of a vital item and thus delaying production. Such a reduction in size of the inventory obviously results in savings.

A third major category of computer applications might be described by the phrase "computing for insight." Most of these applications are probably relevant primarily to scientists and engineers; however, one large group of examples, called *simulations,* are more generally used. For example, an economist who is trying to understand the interplay of a huge number of factors affecting our national economy may be able to create a mathematical model of the economy. In order to investigate the behavior of his model with certain real or assumed input data, he *simulates* the system on a computer. To do this he first produces a computer program which contains steps corresponding to each of the basic relations in his model. For example, his model might assume that a rise in the wages of steelworkers will be reflected in a corresponding increase in the wages of autoworkers. Then the program will contain a subroutine which assigns an increased wage to autoworkers if the input data indicate that steelworkers received an increase during this time period.

After the simulation program has been written, the economist tests it by supplying input data corresponding to real inputs and by allowing the program to run for a time long enough to simulate the operation of the economy during a prescribed period of real time. He can then analyze the behavior of the program to determine whether his model seems to be realistic, i.e., whether the calculated behavior agrees with what actually happened. If it is, he can then simulate the system with other assumed inputs to determine what the model says our economy might do under these conditions. For example, he might supply input data specifying a 10 percent cut in the corporate income tax with all other variables corresponding to actual figures for some year and try to determine what effect such a tax cut would have had.

Programs of this sort are being used to simulate the behavior of a business, or of an entire industry, or of a war! The construction of good models for these purposes is obviously very difficult; however, once a good model has been obtained, it may be possible to obtain more insight into the problem than could possibly be obtained in any other way. A businessman, for example, can simulate what would happen if he decided to double all his prices—if he actually tried it, he might go bankrupt. Simulations are also used to get information about new machines or new processes before they are operational. In addition to providing understanding, such simulations can have great economic value.

As one example of the many ways in which computers are used to gain scientific insight, we shall mention an application to an investigation of visual perception. An experimenter wanted to investigate some proposed models of how the human visual system determines spatial relations, and, in particular, he wanted to eliminate any part of this process which depended on previous knowledge. Such prior knowledge of familiar objects obviously could be important since, for example, when we see something that looks like a house, we have a pretty good idea of its spatial arrangement, no matter what we see. He decided to eliminate this possibility by using various "pseudo-random" patterns of dots as the objects to be examined by the subjects. In order to test various theories as to how binocular vision aids in the perception of depth, he used patterns made up of about 10,000 randomly determined dots; moreover, these patterns were constructed in pairs with one member of the pair having a portion of the pattern slightly displaced from

Figure 11-2   Patterns used by B. Julesz to investigate visual perception.

the other. By using a computer to construct these carefully controlled pseudo-random patterns, he was able to test, and accept or eliminate, a number of conjectures about visual perception. These patterns would have been almost impossible to construct manually, and so such results would have been very difficult, if not impossible, to obtain without the use of the computer. Figure 11-2 shows some of the patterns which were used.

Looking back at our chronology of computer development (page 4), we see that many of the needs which stimulated the early developments required many of the characteristics we have discussed in this chapter. For example, in the eighteenth century, large groups of clerks were employed to calculate, under the direction of a mathematician, very extensive tables of figures which were used for navigation. Following very explicit directions (a program!), the clerks carried out a highly repetitious series of additions and multiplications. Interestingly, it was found that the number of mistakes could be reduced if the clerks had very little mathematical training because they then followed their directions more readily and did not take shortcuts. However, even with very extensive checking it was impossible to eliminate mistakes—many of the mistakes were made in the final step of preparing the printed tables. This need for simple, accurate, and repetitive arithmetic operations and for reliable output stimulated Babbage to design his machine in an attempt to increase the reliability of these tables. In addition, of course, he expected the machine to be less expensive than the large groups of clerks.

Even earlier, weavers of patterned materials had come up against some of these same problems. Before 1750 they had originated the technique of punching holes in cards to specify a pattern. Thus, the first use of symbols stored in punched cards was apparently to represent instructions, not numbers! At first these instructions were simply interpreted by a man, or more likely a boy, and the process was slow, and mistakes were made. A series of modifications to the loom incorporated the punched card more mechanically into the process. The last step was made by Jacquard in 1790 when he produced a very successful loom in which all the power was supplied mechanically and all the control via the punched card. Of course, the card for a particular pattern had to be prepared first by—shall we say—a programmer. In a restricted, but very important, sense the earliest programmable computers were used in process-control applications!

As another example, it was mentioned earlier that Hollerith's work on punched-card machines was stimulated by his realization that it would not be feasible to analyze census data in the time available without some mechanical help.

During the last fifteen years, a continuous stream of new applications has been found. Computers have become faster, cheaper (in terms of equivalent computing capacity), and more reliable, and programmers have vastly improved automatic programming aids. We do not yet see any limits, except those of our own imaginations, to the uses which can be found for computers.

To summarize, we have classified the applications of computers into three categories according to their purpose—economy, feasibility, or insight. Naturally, these are frequently overlapping objectives, but at least one of them is necessary for any fruitful use of computers. One other point should be emphasized; although numbers played some role in most of the applications mentioned, the numbers are, in many ways, incidental. Computers are important today because they can manipulate arbitrary symbols and carry out complex procedures involving many decisions, thus producing economies, or theoretical insight, or doing jobs which would not be feasible without them. Computers are not important just because they can add, subtract, multiply, and divide numbers.

CHAPTER 12

COMPUTER "PRIESTS"

During the Golden Age of Greece, anyone with a tough question to be answered brought it to the oracle at Delphi; no matter how tough the question, the answer was received soon after the question was posed. Although the evidence is somewhat scanty, it appears that the oracle was a priestess who alternately raved and mumbled in a somewhat unintelligible fashion. This priestess was surrounded by a group of priests who "interpreted" her responses as answers to the questions. Apparently, there was always an interpretation which was applicable to the particular problem posed, even though only the priests could find it.

There are some people who feel that the computer is today's oracle and that it operates in much the same fashion as the oracle of Delphi. I do not feel that the analogy is quite that close, but up to this point in our discussion, we have almost completely ignored the fact that computers are surrounded by people. We have seen that they can do marvelous things, but they don't really design or run themselves. Who are the "priests" who make these machines useful? What sort of training do they have? What is the nature of their job?

Perhaps the logical point to begin is with the design and manufacture of a computer. By far the great majority of computer designers are graduate electrical engineers. Many of them have either an

M.S. or a Ph.D. in addition to their bachelor's degree. These people are charged with inventing new devices and circuits. For example, they may be trying to find a cheaper or faster logic gate to perform the AND operation, or they may be trying to find new ways of organizing the circuits in a computer so that fewer circuits are required or so that the overall operation will be faster. In addition to the approximately 5,000 graduate engineers employed in the design and development of computers, probably at least three times as many engineering assistants who do not have college degrees provide them with technical support. The actual production of computers requires more than 60,000 skilled men and women who perform wiring, assembling, or testing tasks similar to those involved in building radios or television sets.

After a computer has been delivered, it is customary for the manufacturer to provide maintenance service for a prescribed monthly fee. The maintenance men almost always have an engineering degree but rarely require advanced degrees. It is their job to carry out daily preventive maintenance tests and, when the machine does develop trouble, to diagnose and repair it. As you can imagine, finding the trouble is usually much harder than fixing it! Since a computer is very expensive and is used for many vital jobs, it is important that these repairs be made in the least possible time. This implies that highly trained maintenance personnel are essential. There are probably about 4,000 people in these jobs at present.

Incidentally, because diagnosing a computer trouble is a very complicated job, the computer itself is used to help! Modern computers are making more and more use of very complicated programs to provide the maintenance man with as much help as possible in locating any trouble in the machine. To go even one level higher—computers are used to develop the programs that computers use to diagnose computers!

With the computer installed and in working order, it is put into operation on a day-to-day basis (and frequently 24 hours per day) by people called, appropriately enough, operators. Keeping the computers operating on all shifts requires about 50,000 operators throughout the country. They are usually high school graduates who have had additional training of from several months to a year in a data-processing–machines course at a technical institute. Some high schools are beginning to offer such training as a part of a vocational course. The operators see that magnetic tape reels are mounted in the tape units when necessary, move decks of punched cards to card readers when this is appropriate, see that printed output gets back to the right person, and occasionally supply some manual inputs to the computer to start it or to get around some difficulty. One of their toughest tasks may be to "schedule" the computer, i.e., decide in what order different jobs should be done so as to get results as fast and efficiently as possible. In addition to the operators, a similar level of training is appropriate for the girls who operate the key punches and other card machines which are frequently used in association with computers. Some 300,000 keypunch operators are already employed in keeping computers supplied with data.

The scheduling task mentioned above is rapidly being taken over at many computer installations by an automatic "operator"—a computer program—which decides in what order all the jobs which have been received should be done. In fact, most installations use such a program, called a *monitor system*, to do many of the things which otherwise would be done by human operators. Such a monitor system can start one job seconds after another is finished, which is much faster than human operators could work. This reduces the lost time between jobs.

By far the largest group of people involved in using computers are the programmers, whose function was discussed in Chapter 10. It has been estimated that there will be 500,000 programmers employed in the United States by 1970. Unfortunately, the word *programmer* is used to refer to a wide range of skills and abilities. At times the word programmer is applied to an expert in mathematics or some field of engineering who has found a way to use a computer to solve one of his problems and has actually written a program to do it. Frequently, such a programmer must have a very thorough knowledge of the problem and possible techniques of solution to solve it even with the aid of the computer. On the other hand, programmer is sometimes used to describe a person who is given a very detailed flow chart and who prepares the list of detailed machine instructions from it. This latter job (which is sometimes called *coding* as distinguished from *programming*) can be performed by high school graduates with additional training in computer programming, whereas the former may be done by someone with a Ph.D. in mathematics or engineering.

Between these two categories we find the bulk of programmers. At present, most of them have a college degree, usually with a major in mathematics. They must be able to understand a problem well enough to produce a flow chart for its solution and also to know the computer well enough to produce an efficient program for its solution.

In the section on programming it was emphasized that compilers and special-purpose languages are being developed to simplify the job of programming. As these techniques develop further, the skills required of programmers will increase. This may seem paradoxical, but the point is that the coding of a program is almost completely eliminated by such techniques whereas each new technique, in the hands of a skilled and imaginative person, allows tougher problems to be tackled. Furthermore, as it becomes easier and easier to program, we find that it is more common for someone with a problem to program it himself rather than to call in a full-time programmer. In my opinion, this trend will continue so that far more than 500,000 people will be programming computers in 1970.

Clearly, the picture of a computer world of the future which requires no people is somewhat overdrawn. There are already hundreds of thousands of people with a variety of skills who are essential to the design, maintenance, operation, and especially the programming of computers. It is the ability of these people to "interpret" the results obtained by computers which makes it the very useful oracle that it is today.

CHAPTER 13

WHAT DOES THE FUTURE HOLD?

There have been a few allusions in the preceding chapters to some likely new developments in computers, and there are so many dramatic and exciting possibilities now in the research stage that it would be a shame not to at least mention them even though it will not be possible to discuss them in much detail. Furthermore, it is in this area that newspaper reporters are sometimes carried away and produce glowing reports that must be accepted with a grain of salt. Perhaps we can present enough information to at least allow reasonable evaluation of such material.

Let's begin with our feet solidly on the ground by mentioning some of the current trends in computer construction. First, engineers are finding ways to make devices smaller and pack them closer together. It is now possible to put as many electronic elements as are in an ordinary television set into a container about the size of the eraser on a pencil. In fact, designers can build several thousand circuits on a chip of material no bigger than a quarter. Their major problem now is finding ways to make connections to these circuits. These integrated circuits and microelectronics are important for several reasons: (1) The speed with which symbols can be transmitted from place to place in the computer has an absolute limit (the speed of light). Reducing the transmission distance is thus the only way to reduce the transmission time and to allow faster computer operation. (2) The sheer bulk of a computer sometimes determines whether it can be used in some applications—for example, in a satellite. (3) Small size usually means that less electrical power is required. Because of these factors, size reductions will make computers faster and more widely applicable. (4) Furthermore, and very important, most of the size-reducing technologies which are being investigated involve "batch processing"; i.e., a large number of devices are made in one operation, and such processes tend to be very economical. This means that computers which are constructed largely of such devices will be cheaper and thus can be economically applied in many more areas.

It seems clear that computers, which have already been drastically reduced in size, will be even further compressed, and it seems that computers of a given complexity will become cheaper. However, don't forget that a computer is no use without input and output equipment, and a pocket-watch computer with a typewriter for a watch fob would be a little inconvenient!

A second major trend is in the use of computers for designing other computers. The design and manufacture of a large computer is a very complicated job which involves a tremendous amount of detail. This makes it well suited to the use of computers, and in the past five years significant portions of the design of new computers have been done on existing computers. This has already tended to reduce the cost of computers (as well as reducing the time and manpower required to develop a new computer), and in the future it may even make custom-designed computers economically feasible and thus further extend their use to situations in which a "special-purpose" computer must be especially designed for a particular application.

The significance of this trend can perhaps be best understood by analogy with the development of the machine-tool industry. In the early stages of the Industrial Revolution, the development of a new machine was a very costly and time-consuming process. Now the modern machine-tool industry can develop the machines for producing a new-model automobile every year—and other less questionable examples of this ability can be given! It is clear that it is this use of machines to make machines which has brought the advantages of mechanization to so many people in so short a time. Similarly, the use of computers to aid in the design of computers reduces the time needed to propagate the application of computers.

A third major trend in computer design today involves experimenting with different machine organizations. The basic organization described here (diagramed in Figure 9-1) has been used by nearly all the machines designed in the last 15 years, although a very large number of different types of devices have been employed. However, designers are now experimenting with many substantially different organizations. One interesting class of organizations being considered involves the use of *multiprocessors,* i.e., instead of one processor unit in the computer, there are two or more. These processors have access to a large memory, and they can all be simultaneously processing parts of one problem or working on different problems. Since the processors share the same memory, the overall configuration provides more computing per dollar than the conventional single-processor organization. Machines of this sort are now being delivered.

Another organization being considered is a highly parallel organization which is made up of thousands of interconnected copies of somewhat simpler machines than the THC 1. Although each machine is relatively limited in capacity, the group can work in parallel on input data and on some problems can effectively speed up processing by many orders of magnitude. This approach has not yet produced any practical systems.

Another interesting organization is based on the use of an *associative* memory, i.e., a memory in which information "associated" with some key or keys could be stored without having to specify a location and then retrieved by referring to one of the keys rather than to a location. Such a memory appears, superficially at least, to be more like human memory, since we do not consciously check a certain "mailbox" in our memories when we are asked, for example, whether it rained last Sunday. Instead we say, "Let's see. Last Sunday I went on a picnic. It rained at the picnic. Yes, it rained last Sunday." In this case, the key that we seemed to search with was *days on which I went on picnics,* or perhaps, *activities last Sunday.* Models of associative memories have been built and are being experimented with at this time.

Concurrently with the pursuit of these new techniques of computer construction, another basic problem is under attack, namely, the obvious difficulty involved in coupling a human being to a machine in which operations are carried on at a rate of millions per second. Elaborate and ingenious equipment is being developed to facilitate information transfer between the user and the machine. Visual displays on a screen very similar to a television screen are one of the most promising tools now under investigation. Under the control of a computer, such screens can display typed information, graphs, drawings of machined parts, circuit diagrams, and many other forms of pictorial information. Obviously, such a display provides output information to the user in a form which has real meaning for him.

In some cases, the computer user is interested in a dynamic process; i.e., the output is changing with time. By using visual displays and the microfilm printer discussed in the chapter on input-output equipment, the computer can be made to produce movies which display the output as it changes. For example, in order to analyze the effect of gyroscopic controls on a satellite's motion, a computer was used to solve the mathematical equations which determine this motion and then to produce a movie showing how the satellite moved around the earth. Figure 13-1 is a composite of many frames of this movie.

In addition to being a very versatile output device, such displays are convenient means of providing input information when they are augmented by a *light pen*. By pointing the light pen at a particular part of the display, the user indicates that he wants to draw a line, erase a character, or take some other action. This technique is likely to be particularly important in applications in which interaction between the computer and the computer user is necessary. Let's consider an example.

In some applications it is not possible to give a precise problem statement and produce a program which will give the solution completely automatically. For example, a designer may have a large number of criteria for evaluating a tentative design but no method of weighing these criteria so that he can objectively specify an optimum. Instead he may want to consider many incomplete, tentative designs and to choose among them on the basis of his engineering judgment. This sort of problem frequently occurs in choosing a particular physical arrangement of the parts of some equipment under design. Visual displays can be prepared by the computer which aid the designer to evaluate the suitability of a placement. By pointing a light pen at the proper place on

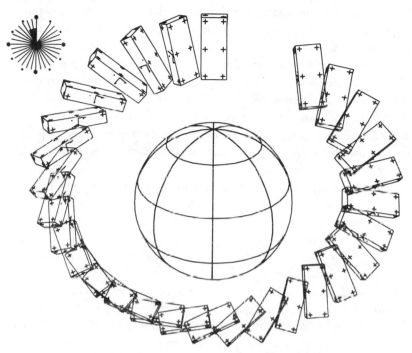

Figure 13-1   Composite of successive frames of a computer-produced movie by Dr. E. E. Zajac entitled "Simulation of Two-Gyro Gravity Gradient Attitude Control System." The box depicts successive positions and orientations of a hypothetical satellite in orbit about the earth.

the screen, he can cause any one of the displays to appear. He can then interchange two parts by pointing the pen at the parts in succession and then by pointing the pen at the word SWAP which appears in the display. The parts are then effectively interchanged, and all displays will now be presented in the correct form with the parts interchanged. A designer is able to try a great many tentative placements in a short time, and thus the computer helps to obtain a better design even though the designer has not specified a simple, precise method of evaluating tentative designs.

Since the designer can make decisions and propose new alternatives at a very slow rate compared with the computer's capacity, it could be very expensive to use a computer in this manner. This has led to another important development, the *time-shared* computer. Experiments are under way in which a single computer is connected to many terminals; some of these terminals are like the visual display described above, and others are simply teletype machines. A user at any of these terminals has the impression that he has the use of an entire machine, but in fact the computer is working for him only a fraction of each second and is doing processing for the other terminals during the remainder of each second. Such arrangements of multiple terminals sharing time on a single main computer seem likely to become very important in the next few years.

Finally, one other important development in improving communication between computers and users should be mentioned. Prior to the extensive use of computers, information was intended solely for examination by people, and consequently it was presented in a form convenient for them. As computers become more and more common, we find that a substantial part of the information with which we are concerned need not ever be processed by a person, and so it should be initially recorded in a form suitable for computer input. This changes the input process drastically, and, in time, it may be difficult to determine just where the computer processing begins and ends. For example, in a department store a sales slip which contains the name of the purchaser, the item purchased, and the amount of the sale is now written out using letters and numbers. If this information is to be processed in a computer for billing or inventory purposes, it has to be laboriously keypunched first. In the near future, this information may be typed at the time of the sale on a machine which will record the transaction directly into a computer memory. As a second example, it is becoming quite common in scientific experiments to completely eliminate the step of recording results as numbers in a book for later analysis. Instead the results are recorded directly on a tape which can be used with no intermediate processing as input to a computer.

Let us move on now to some of the very interesting applications of computers under investigation at present; they stretch the capacity of the computer and the ability of programming techniques to the limits. Games, chess for example, are one example of a variety of "ill-structured" problems which have been tackled. There are two basic difficulties to be met in trying to program a computer to play chess. First, because of the large number of possible moves at each play, there are millions of possible situations resulting from just a few moves. Although the computer is very fast, it is not fast enough to analyze all possible sequences of just five or six moves and still make a move in a reasonable time. Second, not even a chess master can give a precise formula for evaluating the desirability of a certain move; consequently, except for an end game which can be analyzed to a conclusion, it is very difficult to evaluate any strategy.

Since it takes too long to carry out a complete analysis, and a rigorous evaluation of a given move is not possible, the problem is described as *ill-structured*. Such problems have been investigated by writing programs which employ *heuristics*; i.e., the computer carries out a process which seems reasonable but is probably not always optimum. In other words, it uses common sense. Programs of this sort have been written to play poor chess and very good checkers (a better game than the programmer plays), to prove simple theorems in geometry and other branches of mathematics, and to recognize simple patterns. Although some progress is being made, these programs are still quite primitive, and problems of this sort are still not satisfactorily or economically handled by computers. The problems tackled by these heuristic programs provide striking examples of operations which people find quite easy but computers find very difficult. For example, a second grade child can sort out all the letter A's from a large group of badly written letters; a computer is doing well to decide which of two letters is closest to an A if they are not perfectly written.

However, these programs do illustrate very well the point which was made earlier with regard to the machine doing "just what the programmer tells it to do." In the strictest sense of the words, that statement is still true for such programs, but it is just barely true. For example, one of the theorem-proving programs finds proofs for theorems in plane geometry. When asked to prove that the two base angles of an isosceles triangle are equal, the computer produced a proof which was very surprising to the programmer since it was different from, and shorter than, the one usually given in high school textbooks. Of course, if the programmer had sat down and carefully studied what his program would do when given this problem, he could have predicted it would give this proof. However, this might have taken years, and he clearly couldn't do it for all the possible problems which he might try to solve with the program.

Computers are also being used to compose and play music, to write poetry and plays, and to produce pictures. In such applications they are being used sometimes as "instruments" completely controlled by the composer and sometimes as "random elements" which exhibit a degree of novelty or creativity. In one experiment performed recently, a computer was programmed to produce a piece of abstract art very similar to a fairly well-known, and conventionally produced, piece. A survey determined that there was a slight preference for the computer-produced picture when unidentified reproductions of the two pictures were compared. Figure 13-2 shows the computer-produced picture.

Another intriguing possibility which has been intensively investigated is the mechanical translation of documents from one language to another. Since a computer can store a large dictionary of, say, English-Russian synonyms in its memory and since rules of grammar for the two languages can be expressed in a computer program, it seems possible to perform a translation automatically. Programs have been written which produce crude translations which are marginally useful. There are formidable difficulties involved in producing a translation as good as that produced by a competent human translator. This is partly because it has been found that grammarians do not really know what the rules of grammer for any natural language are and partly because a good translation requires that the meaning (semantics) of text be used in making some decisions involved in the process of translation.

Moving on to still another area of current research, many investigators are intrigued by analogies between computers and the human brain and nervous system. Attempts have been made to study the operation of small parts of the brain by using models constructed from devices similar to those used in computers, and, conversely, studies of the mental processing exhibited by humans are being used to guide some computer studies. At present, our knowledge of the physiology involved is quite sketchy—a lot of information has been collected, but much of this is not understood. There are still large gaps in our knowledge—in fact, it is mostly gaps. For example, we know that the brain contains a huge memory, but we do not know just what physical mechanism or mechanisms are involved. We know that specific regions of

Figure 13-2   *Computer composition with lines (1964) by A. Michael Noll.*
    © AMN 1965.

the brain are sometimes involved with specific functions (just as specific circuits in the processor are used in carrying out specific operations), but we do not know the exact nature of this localization of function. We know that chemicals placed in certain parts of the brain of an animal will affect specific behavior, e.g., change the desire for food or water, and that an electrical stimulus can produce similar effects. Thus, we know that both chemical and electrical reactions are involved, but this information is about like that we could obtain by noting the effect on a computer of removing the electric power plug. Although it will undoubtedly take a long time to acquire anything like a reasonably complete understanding of the brain's organization and operation, we shall continue to obtain more and more knowledge through the carefully planned investigations under way in many places.

Many people are also struggling with the question of whether computers "think"; do they have *artificial intelligence*? Probably the toughest part of this question is deciding what it means—what is thinking? Any attempt to define precisely the behavior in a person which could be called thinking usually results either in just listing a set of processes which a computer can obviously do, or in complete frustration. One way around the problem is to define thinking as something which people do, but machines do not do. This simplifies the answer to the question, but it does not provide a very good operational definition.

Of course, many people immediately reject the possibility of computer thinking without even trying to decide what thinking means. This reaction is frequently based on the need to retain the feeling that there must be *something* that people can do that machines cannot. However, in addition to this, there is the feeling that the computer needs a program, and people do not, which implies some sort of superiority. This may be expressed as "The computer does only what some (human) programmer tells it to do."

We have previously commented on this statement and noted that although it is true, it can be very misleading. To carry this discussion a little further, is it true that a person is not "programmed"? We send our children to school to receive quite detailed and specific instruction for many hours. In addition, the child sees and hears a great many other things which act as instructions. Thus, although his instructions are very complicated, are received over long periods of time from many sources, and are highly interrelated, they do constitute a very large program. In many, or perhaps most, situations in which we think a child has done something it was not "told to do," an extensive analysis of his background and training might make his action seem very routine. Notice that this argument is not denying the possibility of some process taking place in the brain which is qualitatively different from any process taking place in a computer. It simply states that a great many human actions which seem surprising are no more surprising than computer results obtained by using a complicated program which cannot be examined.

Since it is very hard, if not impossible, to get a good operational definition of thinking, we cannot come to any definitive conclusion as to whether computers think. However, it is clear that, no matter whether computers do or do not think, computers and people are best suited to do different things in different ways. Computers are far faster than people in doing many operations, e.g., adding numbers, and, barring a totally unforeseen evolutionary change, this will never be changed. On the other hand, people are much better than computers at recognizing patterns. Although it is conceivable that some day a computer could be equipped with suitable input equipment and a suitable program so that it could recognize a face in a crowd, it is quite unlikely that it will ever be able to outdo a one- or two-year old child in this respect. Many more examples could be given, but it seems unnecessary to belabor the fact that some problems are better suited to one than to the other.

Thinking is sometimes tied to the process of learning (which also is hard to define). Consequently, there is a lot of interest in programs that "learn," i.e., in some sense or another they perform better after they have been used a number of times. In many situations this is easy to do by simply allowing certain parameters of the program to depend on previous runs and/or by storing results from previous runs in memory. A very good checker-playing program has been written which functions in this manner.

Closely related to the idea of a learning program is that of an *adaptive system*. An adaptive system has the characteristic that it changes its operation (it is hoped in such a way as to improve it) as a result of input information which indicates that its performance is improving or worsening. It is not too difficult to obtain this sort of effect if the system has a few adjustable parameters built into it. However, no one has yet discovered any type of device which is suitable for economically constructing computers and which is such that major changes in the system organization can be "adaptively" obtained. It seems unlikely that any substantial widening of computer applications will be obtained in this way.

To conclude this section, perhaps we should mention the idea of a *self-reproducing system.* It has been shown to be logically possible to construct a machine which contains its own description so that it can copy itself; i.e., it would be self-reproducing. Naturally, such a machine would need a source of energy and raw materials—it has been suggested that perhaps the easiest way to make these available would be to have this machine exist in the sea. Although some people feel that it would be technically feasible to produce such a machine within a matter of a decade or so, my own opinion is that they won't be here within 20 years. After that?

CHAPTER 14

1984?

The extremely rapid emergence of computers as an important element in our society has made many people apprehensive of their effects. Along with other stress-producing developments such as the invention of nuclear and other super weapons, a rapidly increasing world population, tremendously increased speeds of transportation and communication, and others, computers are making Orwell's *1984* seem less and less like a bad dream and more and more like a reasonable prediction. Clearly, we cannot have a lot of confidence in any concrete predictions about what will happen in the future since the actions taken by people as a result of their hopes and fears have a great deal to do with determining what happens. However, we can point out some of the forces and the resulting stresses and perhaps increase the likelihood of a favorable course of action.

Certainly the most discussed problems at this time are those due to the economic implications of computers. Do computers increase or decrease unemployment? Will computers improve our standard of living, or will they condemn a large segment of our society to substandard living conditions because they cannot find work? The answers to these and similar questions are being debated vociferously at present. There are some (for example, the Committee on the Triple Revolution) who feel strongly that computers will very soon reduce the work force required to maintain our standard of living to a small fraction of the available working population. Others (for example, *Fortune* magazine's C. E. Silberman) feel that the effect on employment has been, and will continue to be, much less drastic. Who is right? Nobody knows.

Certainly, if we examine what has actually been happening, we can agree on a few things. First, *automation,* or the process of mechanizing productive work, does not involve just computers; it includes the development of machinery for simplifying or speeding up any part of the process. Such developments, for example, machine tools, construction equipment, long antedate the existence of digital computers. Second, digital computers are able to do many jobs which we formerly assumed could be done only by people since they involved some mental as well as physical effort. Consequently, there no longer appear to be any intrinsic bounds, except for economic ones, on the possibility of automating nearly all jobs. Third, although in a relatively few instances a computer installation has resulted in some people actually losing their jobs, in most instances these people are retained by the same company. They do either completely new jobs or work that wasn't economical to attempt to do before, but is now, or else they supplement workers who are doing jobs which it is not economical to automate and thus enable the company to meet a greater demand for its products. Employment figures over the period during which computers have been commercially available clearly indicate that, *up to now,* computers have not been responsible for unemployment.

What are some of the advantages and disadvantages of automation for the affected employees? Generally speaking, working conditions are improved; the environment tends to be cleaner, safer, and more pleasant to work in. On the other hand, there is some evidence that the mental tensions associated with the job increase—partly because of greater isolation from other employees. Automation generally requires a large amount of training in new skills (in some cases 90 percent of the employees had to develop new skills) but usually with no significant increase in the level of the skills. However, there are usually new jobs created, which are frequently filled by hiring new employees rather than by retraining, which require higher skills so that the average level of training is increased.

How does automation affect the consumer? If we want everybody to get higher wages without prices rising accordingly, i.e., if we want a higher standard of living, then it is clear that we must use fewer people to do a job. For example, if we do not find some way to reduce the number of clerks required to produce your light bill; then your bill must go up if their wages are to go up. Thus, increasing our standard of living depends, to a large extent, on not eliminating automation.

Now, how about the future? Maybe few people are fired, but if we can produce more and more goods with the same number of people, where will the jobs for our larger working population come from? Here the atmosphere gets a little foggy. Evidence from the recent past indicates that we can expect a continually increasing fraction of our work force to go into services such as teaching, nursing, barbering, etc. In fact, by 1963 the number of people employed in service industries was greater (60 percent) than the number of workers employed in the production of goods. This is a rather remarkable change considering that as late as 1900, 65 percent of the work force was employed in production activities. This seems to be an important way in which increasing mechanization can make possible a higher standard of living for everyone.

In addition to this big increase in the number of service jobs, there are factors tending to increase employment in production industries. For example, surveys indicate consumer demand is not saturated even at annual family incomes of around $30,000 which is approximately six times the average annual family income. However, some people feel that eventually either the average workweek will have to be drastically reduced, or we shall have to accept the fact that a large part of our potential work force will do no productive work but will be supported by an "aristocracy" of workers. Clearly, either of these alternatives would lead to severe difficulties in keeping people's leisure time occupied and in avoiding strains due to different classes of workers. However, it is hard to believe that a real effort to find some way for everybody to make a useful contribution to society could fail. There seems to be a logical inconsistency in the picture of many people sitting around with nothing satisfying to do when they are free to do whatever they wish.

In addition to the economic problems related to the introduction of computers, there are many others of some concern. For example, to what extent are computers dehumanizing people? Clearly, a banker is not likely to feel quite the same way about 7136542, whom he never sees, as he is about Harry Jones, who stops in each week to make a deposit. A draftsman doesn't get the same satisfaction out of supplying a few punched cards to a computer program as he does out of producing an elegant drawing of a complicated assembly of equipment. The computer running a telephone office can't please you with congratulations on your new baby the way Mabel used to. Are we all going to become just numbers?

Although problems such as the above are certainly real and are becoming important to more and more people, there are a number of factors which are not quite so obvious that tend in the other direction. For one thing, the companies which are automating many of their contacts with customers are quite conscious of the fact that the impersonal, mechanical contact may lead to trouble. Consequently, in many instances they are attempting to use the automated systems to provide new services and more individual attention than was feasible formerly. For example, by using terminals which are connected to a time-shared computer, a bank clerk may be able to give a nearly instantaneous response to a query about an account balance, whereas before, the customer would have had to wait until the end of the month. Or perhaps the clerk whose job was taken over by a computer will be put to work expediting the special treatment needed for an order by a new customer. All in all, it is certainly possible for better and more individual attention to result from a computer installation.

Because of the difficulty in communication between man and machine, it has been true that, after a computer program was written, there was very little creativity required, or personal satisfaction obtained, in using that program. It almost always requires simply providing some punched cards or other form of data along with the program. Of course, the preparation of the program can be a very challenging and stimulating task which provides a great deal of personal satisfaction. (To digress a moment, many computer programmers are prima donnas who are temperamentally more akin to artists than to technicians.) Some of the developments which were discussed in the last chapter promise to change this situation considerably. A user who sits at a visual display and cooperates with the computer in manipulating a tentative equipment design until a satisfactory one is obtained gets a very real feeling of accomplishment. He is using a powerful tool and obtains just as tangible results as the operator of a large bulldozer or power shovel. Incidentally, he may also attract a group of sidewalk superintendents while he is working! As we find better and better ways of communicating with computers, it appears likely that the most economical way of doing many jobs will involve such interaction between men and computers with the result that a feeling of definite personal satisfaction will be obtained by the men. I can't say whether the same is true for the machines!

A somewhat more nebulous question might be phrased as "Who's in control—computers or people?" People are concerned, for example, as to whether the use of computers in military systems may make a nuclear war more likely or whether the rapidity with which changes can be introduced may lead to actions which are socially or politically unwise. One answer, which sounds facetious but is usually intended seriously, is "We can always pull the plug." This answer is very misleading, or naïve, for several reasons. First, systems which incorporate computers can either make or require a person to make decisions in a very short time. If a weapon system can detect, analyze, and react to an attack within 15 minutes, it probably will not be employed in a manner which allows several days' debate about what action should be taken. It does no good to pull a plug once a decision has been forced. Second, people in important political, military, or industrial positions may be nearly completely isolated from the basic data which is supplied to sophisticated data-processing systems. As a consequence, the picture they see and the decisions they make could be remote from reality even though their own impression might be that "Everything is fine; don't pull any plugs." Of course, this is not new; administrators have always been faced with this problem. However, computers depend so heavily on the abstract model which is used to plan the processing, and they enable such vast quantities of data to be processed, that the problem is much, much bigger.

The question of control has not always been a primary concern of individuals; historically, many societies just accepted the existing power structure as the natural one. However, a modern free society maintains a continuous struggle to see that control is not obtained by one individual, or group of individuals, such as the military, or the business community, or a labor group, or a group of politicians. The structure of our society is already so complex that it is very difficult to unravel the control mechanisms and determine where dangers exist. These problems are undoubtedly going to be even harder as computers take over more and more functions.

To consider a simple example of this sort, let us suppose that we eventually use computers to record and total the vote in a national election. How can we ensure that the result is "honest"? As a more extreme example, assume that a computer is used to search through a legal code and records of previous decisions to prepare briefs for a judge or perhaps even to make the judicial decision, how can we analyze the program to determine that it is "unbiased"? These same problems exist at present, but we have a great deal of applicable experience to help us in solving them. Clearly, we shall have to proceed cautiously and build up comparable experience as we introduce computers into such activities.

My own opinion with respect to all of these questions is that the computer has had, and will continue to have, a large net positive value. For every serious problem which they raise, it is possible to formulate methods (usually using computers) which appear to alleviate the problem and result in a net improvement in the situation. Many other, probably all other, important and valuable technological developments have brought serious problems with them. Are computers a menace to society? They could be, but books could also be a menace to society.* It has been pointed out that any tool that is sharp enough to be useful is sharp enough to hurt. It seems to boil down to this—if computers are used properly, they will be a tremendous boon to mankind; if they are used improperly, they will do serious harm. And this statement, of course, can be made about every important element of any society, past or present.

* Many people, especially many mathematicians, have expressed the fear that computer users will lose their analytic powers. The following quotation from Plato indicates that similar fears are not new. "Said Thoth to the King of Egypt, 'This invention, O King, will make the Egyptians wiser and will improve their memories; for it is an elixir of memory and wisdom that I have discovered,' but the king was not convinced and feared that the invention of writing would impair the memory instead of improving it and that the people would read without understanding."

If we assume that this feeling is correct and that the effects of computers are neither inevitably good nor bad, but depend on their use, an important conclusion can be drawn. It is important that a reasonably good basic understanding of the functioning and use of computers should be a part of everybody's general body of knowledge in order to maximize the possible benefits and minimize the possible harm. Debates such as those attending the widely publicized congressional hearings on a proposed national data center will almost inevitably arise over whether a certain use is good or bad. It is important that decisions be made on the basis of some understanding rather than by some completely irrational process. Such understanding hasn't prevented our making mistakes in the past, and undoubtedly it is no guarantee for the future, but at least it leaves room for hope. It has been my hope and intention that this book would provide an adequate basic understanding to meet this need.

SELECTED GENERAL
BIBLIOGRAPHY ON COMPUTERS

Adler, I: *Thinking Machines*, John Day, New York, 1961. 189 pages. A layman's introduction to logic, Boolean algebra, and computers.

Andrew, A. M.: *Brains and Computers*, Harrap, Toronto, 1963. 78 pages. Very simple introduction to computers. Most of the book is devoted to description of the brain.

Arden, B. W.: *An Introduction to Digital Computing*, Addison-Wesley, Reading, Mass., 1963. 389 pages. An introductory text based on an undergraduate course. Both programming language and machine design are treated.

Arnold, P., and P. White: *The Automation Age*, Holiday, New York, 1963. 197 pages. An extremely readable survey of computers and automation, with many examples of automation at work.

Berkeley, E. C.: *The Computer Revolution*, Doubleday, Garden City, N.Y., 1962. 249 pages. An account of the effects of the computer on information processing. It includes a short history of computers and contemplates their future applications.

Bernstein, Jeremy: *The Analytical Engine*, Random House, New York, 1963. 113 pages. Reprint of two articles from the *New Yorker* magazine. Very good but brief introduction to computers and programming.

Calingaert, P.: *Principles of Computation*, Addison-Wesley, Reading, Mass., 1965. 200 pages. Introduction to numerical analysis. Short history of computers and brief section on analog computation. Undergraduate textbook.

Desmonde, W. H.: *Computers and Their Uses,* Prentice-Hall, Englewood Cliffs, N.J., 1964. 296 pages. A comprehensive introduction to computers. It introduces Turing machines and automata theory.

General Electric: *You and the Computer,* 1965. 21 pages. A good, simple introduction to computers, intended for high school students.

Haas, G.: *Design and Operation of Digital Computers,* Sams and Bobbs-Merrill, Indianapolis and New York, 1963. 272 pages. A comprehensive survey of fundamentals, components, and circuits used in computers. The fundamentals are presented at an elementary level. The rest of the book is considerably more technical and will appeal to readers with some electronics background.

IBM: *General Information Manual,* 1960. 95 pages. An introduction to IBM data-processing systems.

McCormick, E. M.: *Digital Computer Primer,* McGraw-Hill, New York, 1959. 214 pages. A presentation of the basic principles of computer design and applications. It is intended to provide general background material for anyone who is interested in computers.

Pfeiffer, J. P.: *The Thinking Machine,* Lippincott, Philadelphia, 1962. 242 pages. Based on a television program, this book constitutes a very readable introduction to the workings, accomplishments, and future possibilities of electronic computers.

Philipson, Morris (ed.): *Automation: Implications for the Future,* Vintage Books, New York, 1962. A collection of essays in implications for labor, industry, social sciences, education, leisure, government. Not bad.

Quinn, F. X. (ed.): *The Ethical Aftermath of Automation,* Newman, Westminster, Md., 1962. 270 pages. Proceedings of a seminar on automation and its effects. Articles are of mixed quality. Report of President's Commission in an appendix. Good bibliography.

Schultz, Louise: *Digital Processing: A System Orientation,* Prentice-Hall, Englewood Cliffs, N.J., 1963. 400 pages. Part I, Numerical Notation and Arithmetic; Part II, History and Applications; Part III, Organization and Programming. A well-written book. Contains a good bibliography.

INDEX

Catalog

If you are interested in a list of fine Paperback
books, covering a wide range of subjects
and interests, send your name and address,
requesting your free catalog, to:

McGraw-Hill Paperbacks
330 West 42nd Street
New York, New York 10036